# MEMORIES OF
# CON HOWARD

A COLLECTION OF TRIBUTES TO THE LATE, GREAT CON HOWARD,
FROM THE PEOPLE WHO KNEW HIM BEST.

EDITED BY MARY CAULFIELD

# MEMORIES OF
# CON HOWARD

© The Contributors 2012

All rights reserved. No part of this publication may be reproduced in any form or by any means without the prior permission of the publisher or else under the terms of a licence permitting photocopying issued by the Irish Copyright Licensing Agency or a similar reproductive rights organisation. British Library Cataloguing-in-Publication data is available for this book.

ISBN NO: 978-0-9553419-8-4

First published in 2012 by Hot Press Books,
13 Trinity St.,
Dublin 2,
Ireland.
Available to purchase from www.hotpress.com/shop

Design: David Keane
Production Manager: Mairin Sheehy
Typesetting: Maeve Heslin
Studio Manager: Graham Keogh
Front cover photograph by John Horgan, reproduced with permission from Clare County Library. Back cover photograph is of Con with his granddaughter Nicola.

All rights reserved. No part of this publication may be reproduced or transmitted in any form or by any means electronic or mechanical, including photocopying, recording or any information retrieval system without the prior permission of the publisher, in writing.

Printed and bound by Gemini International.

For Con's beloved sister Kathleen Hurley

"And all that's best of dark and bright
Meet in her aspect and her eyes".

Lord Byron

# CON HOWARD

Con Howard was born in Dysart, Co. Clare in 1925. He was educated at St. Flannan's College in Ennis, Trinity College, Dublin, and the London School of Economics. Con's wife Margery died shortly after him. He is survived by his children Conor, Hilary, Patricia, Aileen, Áine and Morgan. Con was a career diplomat. He was consul general in Boston and press counsellor in the Irish Embassies in Washington and London, and secretary of the delegation to the Council of Europe in Strasbourg and Paris. He was founder of Cumman Merriman, the British Irish Association, the Society of St. Brendan and the Irish-Australian conference for the Australian Centennial. After retirement, he was honorary consul for Sri Lanka in Ireland. He was vice president of the United Arts Club.

# MEMORIES OF CON HOWARD

## CONTENTS

| | |
|---|---|
| Foreword | 11 |
| 'Diplomacy – Irish Style': *The Guardian*, July 14, 1972 | 13 |
| John Banville: 'Some Guy' | 14 |
| John Behan: Green Be His Memory | 16 |
| Maeve Binchy: Anything Was Possible With Con | 17 |
| Wesley Boyd, 'An Irishman's Diary': *The Irish Times*, August 18, 2010 | 19 |
| Patricia Boylan: An extract from her book *All Cultivated People*, by kind permission of the Boylan family, and publisher Colin Smythe | 22 |
| Dominick Lord Oranmore and Browne: Clare Man | 24 |
| Pat Byrne: In Memory Of Con Howard | 27 |
| Mary Caulfield: Con And The United Arts Club | 29 |
| Brendan Conway: A Hoary Old Celt | 32 |
| Anthony Cronin: Structures Of Lasting Value Sprang From The Ground He Trod | 35 |
| Seán Donlon: A True Patriot | 38 |
| James Downey: An extract from his book *In My Own Time*, by kind permission of the author | 41 |
| Desmond Fennell: Filled With Ireland | 42 |
| Seamus Heaney: The Disappearing Island | 44 |
| Monica Henchy: A Faithful Visitor | 45 |
| Nuala Hogan: A Wicked Sense Of Humour | 47 |
| Catherine Jennings: Travels With Con And The Brendan Society | 49 |
| Joseph Judge: A Letter To Con Howard | 55 |

| | |
|---|---|
| Morgan Llywelyn: A Complex Individual | 58 |
| Brendan Lynch: A Man Of Myriad Enthusiams | 62 |
| Peadar Mac Mághnais: The Spirit Of Merriman | 64 |
| Seán Mac Mathúna: Where The Waters Fall | 70 |
| Derek Mahon: An Indian Garden | 74 |
| Brian Mooney: The One That Got Away | 76 |
| Mike Mooney: Carousing On Capitol Hill | 78 |
| Brendan Ó Cathaoir: A Clare Man Through And Through | 81 |
| Ulick O'Connor: A Celtic Prince Out For A Walk | 84 |
| Aidan O'Hara: He Made The Best Of This | 86 |
| Seán Ó Mordha: An Ideal Man | 87 |
| Rosemarie Rowley: For Con Howard | 89 |
| Desmond Rushe: A Born Communicator | 90 |
| Rose Rushe: Viva, Meh-ico | 93 |
| Bob Ryan: An extract from his book *With A Tap On The Knee* by kind permission of the author | 100 |
| Tom Stack: A Romantic Par Excellence | 105 |
| Mary Stokes: Con And The Society Of St. Brendan | 108 |
| Richard Stokes: Con And Sir Sidney Nolan | 111 |
| Sean Tyrrell: The Midnight Court | 113 |
| Gabriel Rosenstock: 'A Haiku For Con' (Picture, page 1) | |
| The Contributors | 117 |
| Acknowledgements | 125 |

# FOREWORD

Memories of Con Howard, diplomat, bon viveur, original thinker, balladeer...

To say that Con was multi-talented is an understatement. He was founder of the British-Irish Association, as well as a host of cultural organisations ranging from St. Brendan to Brian Merriman. He was also variously Editor-in-Chief of the prize-winning *American And Ireland 1776 – 1976*, and Organiser-in-Chief of major conferences on America and Australia; Saviour of the Shaw House and Patron Saint of the United Arts Club; and Spiritual Guide on hilarious tours of the United States, Australia, Paris, Iona, and the Mexico of the San Patricios. Through all the fun, there was a common theme running through Con's inspirations – the crucial importance of the Diaspora as a valuable national resource. As you will see over the following pages, in so many ways, Con Howard was ahead of his time.

In these Memories, Con becomes his admirers.

Ní bheidh a leithéid arís ann.

– Peadar Mac Mághnais

# 'DIPLOMACY – IRISH STYLE':
*The Guardian*, July 14, 1972

Con Howard, press counsellor at the Irish Embassy in London, and probably one of the best known of the diplomatic press corps, is being sent from London to Boston as Irish Consul General, one of the diplomatic surprises of the season.

Diplomats come and go, of course. Howard, though, has made his presence felt in a way few others have matched. He won the respect of the Foreign Office as a force to be reckoned with – and the regret, on occasion, of his counterparts at the former Ulster Office, who could never quite match his cultural barrage. There are queues of British and foreign television and film people who have found themselves packed off to look at West of Ireland high crosses, festivals, literary legends and tales of country folk. It is one reason for the marked Republican sympathies of the London-based European press.

Politically, Fleet Street was treated to the (diplomatically) rare delights of open debate with Unionists (notably John Taylor, at one famous party conference) and British Tories. Not usual diplomatic method, but then the Irish Embassy had almost no contact with the press before Howard arrived and the last three years of Anglo-Irish relations have taken the propaganda war far beyond the cocktail party circuit.

Howard was formerly the Irish Vice-Consul in Boston. There is some logic in sending him back, after establishing his reputation in London. Some of his friends in London and Dublin, though, have been appalled at the decision to cut short his work in London and have protested quietly to the Irish Foreign Affairs Department.

## JOHN BANVILLE
'Some Guy'

One day in the 1990s, I was travelling in a taxi in Washington DC. I noticed that the taxi-man, a middle-aged, tough-looking number in a baseball cap, was eyeing me with lively surmise in the driving mirror. 'You're Irish, yeah?' he said. I admitted I was. He grinned. 'You know a guy called Con Howard?' Startled, I said that I did, indeed. 'Some guy, that guy,' the driver murmured, with a wondering shake of the head. 'Yeah, some guy.'

It is surely a mark of special renown to be remembered by name by a taxi driver in one of the central hubs of the world. Through the years, how many politicians and diplomats, of every class, colour and creed, must my man have ferried to and fro through the grid of Washington's streets? At one time or other he had probably had a few Kennedys in the back, some Bushes and assorted shrubs, a Kissinger, a Cheney, a Rumsfeld… even, perhaps, a Haughey. But it was Con Howard he recalled, even though Con had not served in Washington since the beginning of the 1980s.

It is hard to avoid the clichés. He was a 'character'. He was larger than life. He was a broth of a boy. He was *from Clare*, for heaven's sake! Yet for all his boisterousness it is clear that he was a skilled and subtle diplomat, and a persuasive ambassador for Ireland in London, Boston, Washington, albeit one with a lower-case *a*. No doubt the case would have been raised to upper had he been less colourful and irrepressible – had he been, that is, a bit of a drudge. But Con was never one to pass up the chance of cakes and ale, and to hell with the puritans.

Along with his exploits abroad, his driving role in the cultural life of this country is well known. He invented the summer school, with the founding of An Cumann Merriman back in the 1960s, and forged strong cultural links with America, Australia, Britain and numerous other European countries. And who but Con Howard would have ended up as the Sri Lankan honorary consul to Ireland?

Yeah, some guy.

## JOHN BEHAN
Green Be His Memory

Con Howard? What can I say of such a phenomenon? Long before I met Con in the Arts Club, I had heard of him from Eddie Linden in London – Eddie sang his praises. Con was instrumental in promoting Eddie's magnificent literary magazine *Aquarius* when it most needed support, in its first faltering steps, for as Brendan Behan remarked, "All beginnings are weak".

As a result of that inspired support, Eddie and his dedicated friends and advisors have published, over four decades, some of the best poetry and prose, with supporting drawings, to be witnessed anywhere in the world.

The list of prose writers, poets and visual artists is remarkable, a who's who of modern art: Seamus Heaney, Anthony Cronin, Ralph Steadman, John Heath-Stubbs, Robert Creeley, Gerald Mangan, John Minihan, the list is endless; consult 'Eddie's own Aquarius' for a full list.

Con Howard's enthusiasm for all things cultural knew no bounds. His range of interest was wide and varied, and included music, history, literature and the visual arts, and all things Clare. Green be his name and green be his memory.

# MAEVE BINCHY
Anything Was Possible With Con

All of Con Howard's friends, and we are many, remember the laughs, the enthusiasms, the belief that anything was possible. Those are the stories that are always told about him and will be told for decades ahead.

But not everyone knows the serious side of Con, his values and his strong belief that being Irish was hugely important and brought with it not only rights but also responsibilities.

I came across this in London once during one of the many Irish bank strikes. These bank strikes, which were wonderful and liberating for the rest of us, were a bit worrying for those who had actually worked in a bank. Many of them went to London to get temporary jobs.

Con worked in the Irish Embassy in London at that time, and, being Con, he got to know many of the bank workers and often helped them to find work. It was a time when it was quite easy for anyone with experience working in a bank to walk into an office job in London. But often they landed in desperate places and started thinking about leaving.

One evening I was in a bar with Con and two very unhappy campers came in. One was a woman working as a telephonist in a law office where everyone called each other Mr. this and Mr. that, and where a great cloud of silence hung over the whole place. There were four major feuds going on – and this partner must not be connected by phone to that partner, and there were arguments every day about the tea and biscuits, and who had contributed to what. Naturally she hated it and was about to walk out, but Con begged her not to. "We don't want these people to say that the Irish are just like the stereotype, feckless and unreliable. Go on, try to stick it out for the week and then we'll find something better."

Then this man came in with his story of a temporary job in a fish shop. The couple that ran it hadn't a clue. They were charmless to the customers, and inefficient in their pricing. They were barely making any profit and the place could have been a gold mine. He couldn't bear it for another day.

"Just don't abandon them," Con begged. "Help them. Turn them round, let them always remember the summer they had this marvellous Irishman working with them when things suddenly took a turn for the better."

The woman went back to the law office and stuck the week out. She says that they hardly noticed whether she was there or not, but they said goodbye graciously enough, so at least Con had won that battle to make the Irish seem less unreliable than we are. And the man in the fish shop *did* in fact turn the place around and smartened it all up with lovely murals of fishy scenes and special carrier bags with a logo on them. In fact he never went back to the bank. He married the daughter of the house and still lives happily in his fish empire, where his sons are training to work in the business.

And Con, whose life always seemed on the surface to be an endless pursuit of fun and laughter, yet again managed to do good for Ireland and its image. It was just two people on that one evening, but there were many, many more.

Con Howard's legacy lives on in ways that none of us will ever really know about. The stories are all out there somewhere.

# WESLEY BOYD
'An Irishman's Diary': *The Irish Times*, August 18, 2010

The father of all the summer schools, Merriman, starts its annual gathering in Ennis today, for the first time without its own founding father, the rumbustious Con Howard. It was 43 years ago that Con, with a jovial band of locals and aliens, established the school to commemorate the work of the 18th century Clare poet, Brian Merriman, and, in particular, his great racy poem, *The Midnight Court* – described by a regular at the school, Prof. Séan Ó Tuama, as "certainly the greatest comic poem ever written in Ireland."

As a professional diplomat, Con wandered to many lands, but he remained connected to his native Co. Clare by an unyielding umbilical cord. Right up to his death at the age of 84 in October last year he was arranging to organise yet another festival in the county to mark the glorious battle of 1318 in his native Dysart.

Con Howard was no ordinary diplomat. Adventurous, innovative, bold and boisterous, he made friends and influenced people in many countries, particularly the United States and Britain. His unorthodox style did not always endear him to his supervisors in Iveagh House, and no Minister for Foreign Affairs was courageous enough to appoint him to an ambassadorship, a rank that he truly merited and would have filled with élan and dynamism.

Who but this ebullient Clareman could count among his friends the heavyweight champion of the world, Rocky Marciano, the Australian painter, Sir Sidney Nolan, and a British Prime Minister, Ted Heath? After a period in the cultural section of the Department of Foreign Affairs, where he was inspirational in promoting Ireland through film and literature, he spent five years in the consulate in Boston.

He and his wife Margery (who sadly died a few weeks after Con) quickly established themselves on the city's social and political circuits.

Con was one of the first to steer official America away from the green-tinted images of paddywackery and begorrah and to view Ireland as a fertile ground for industrial and business investment. He became a close friend of the Kennedys and other east coast politicians, and began to plant the positive seeds that eventually led to the establishment of "the Four Horsemen" (Tip O'Neill, Pat Moynihan, Ted Kennedy and Hugh Carey). This early work was developed further when he returned to Boston years later as consul general after service in Dublin and London. Con ploughed a wide field of political, sporting and academic contacts, and gained public recognition beyond the confines of his office. Tip O'Neill, the Speaker of the House, remarked at dinner: "If Con Howard and I stood for Mayor of Boston tomorrow, Con would win."

Con excelled as press counsellor at the embassy in London. Ambassadors would spend months endeavouring to get editors of national papers to come to lunch or dinner. Con discovered that editors, like most journalists, enjoyed nothing better than a pint and a chat during breaks in production. He was a frequent visitor to the pubs of Fleet Street. In the King And Keys he became a firm friend of Bill Deedes, the editor of the *Daily Telegraph* and in Mooneys' Irish House he was made welcome by Stafford Somerfield, the editor of the *News Of The World*.

Concerned at the influence he was wielding, the Unionist government at Stormont recruited one of the best journalists in the North, Tommie Roberts, the political correspondent of the *Belfast Telegraph,* as press officer in the Ulster Office in London to counter Con's work. They were soon good friends. (Tommie was rewarded with a knighthood: Con spent years of his retirement fighting a fruitless legal battle with Iveagh House for compensation for a fall on government premises.)

When he was posted from London to Boston, a columnist in the *Guardian* commented: "Howard has made his presence felt in a way few others have matched. He won the respect of the Foreign Office as a force to be reckoned with – and the regret, on occasion, of his counterparts at the former Ulster Office, who could never quite match his cultural barrage."

After Boston, Con had a final posting in the United States as press counsellor at the embassy in Washington, reporting to the ambassador, Seán Donlon. He supported Donlon's efforts, often unpopular, to swing Washington behind the campaign to find a peaceful solution in Northern Ireland with the help of the Four Horsemen.

Away from his official duties, Con harnessed his relentless energy to many initiatives of benefit to the nation as a whole, and especially to his native Clare. As well as being the founding force in establishing the Merriman Summer School, he set up the Society of St. Brendan to travel to strange places. With the able assistance of Mary Caulfield he struggled to keep the Arts Club in Dublin alive through a period of lean years. Little excuse was needed to organise a group of like minds for excursions from the club to Berlin to commemorate the 100th anniversary of the translation of *Cúirt An Mhean Oíche* into German, to Mexico to celebrate the San Patricio Brigade of Irish soldiers who fought against the Americans, to Paris for Bastille Day, to Iona for pilgrimages. In a tribute at his funeral the writer, Ulick O'Connor, recalled seeing Con a few weeks before his death in the streets of Dublin on his walking stick "striding out like a Celtic prince among his people."

## PATRICIA BOYLAN
An extract from *All Cultured People*

The 75th anniversary of the United Arts Club loomed and a solitary force dedicated to the task was required to get a programme worthy of old ghosts under way. Mere ebullience would not do. Exuberance was necessary. Con Howard, a man from Co. Clare, stepped forward. The *Concise Oxford English Dictionary* defines 'exuberant' in part as "luxuriantly prolific… overflowing with spirits (of language)": he is this and more. Howard is an ornament of the Department of Foreign Affairs and an adopted son of Irish America since his sojourn in Boston as Irish Consul-General and his stint in Washington. In 1982 he was a picador member of the Club Committee. He was the only begetter of the national, popular and successful 'Cumann Merriman'. He founded the Brendan Society, incorporating a concept of an Irish university of the sea, and he initiated the British Irish Association, created for the betterment of relations between Britain and Ireland. (He even hoped to persuade Mrs. Thatcher to visit the Club.) His project for 1988, to claim Australia for the Irish in celebration of its Centennial, has been partly successful.

To him must go the credit for the conception of the brilliant series of events (most of which took place!) celebrating the Club's 75th anniversary. But for him the date might have passed unnoticed and the torpor of age allowed, unhindered, the sad decline of the Arts part of a Club only sporadically United in the 'promotion of all the Arts of painting and literature, poetry and music.' Passion was all but spent when Con girded himself for the hundred or so battles against antipathy and produced his ambitious programme.

Dr. Seoirse Bodley began it in November with a concert, the

second half of which was a first performance of his song cycle, *A Girl*, with poems by Brendan Kennelly, and sung by the Irish/American mezzo-soprano, Aylish Kerrigan. Benedict Kiely, that master storyteller, read 'Bloodless Byrne Of A Monday', specially written for the occasion, at a literary luncheon. Amusement was almost submerged in delight at the rise and fall of the well-paced cadences. Seamus Heaney read some of his poems at another luncheon, when he sat on after the meal and discoursed with wit and warmth with all who approached him, as everyone did. Cyril Cusack read his own inspired selection from the poetry of WB Yeats, and the packed audience stayed on for a talk on the genesis of the Club and its foundation. Kiely, Heaney, and Cusack! Three shining stars in a matter of days! Old ghosts, if they listened, must have purred, especially Ellie Duncan's.

Published by kind permission of the Boylan family and publisher Colin Smythe.

## DOMINICK LORD ORANMORE AND BROWNE
'Clare Man'

Con Howard Clare man born.
Had no fear of the present storm
escaped from Clare to the Dublin streets.
Honesty, truth, bled from his solid feet.
Con famed with the Washington elite,
his sincerity, laughter, people weep.
Unique character, Con's memory we keep.

You find characters in their dozens. Many make it to fame or disrepute, and their names go down in Irish history, others are not forgotten for their many qualities, their extraordinary character and inexhaustible energy, their stardom and their special value of heart and human kindness.

Con Howard was a man from Co. Clare, born in Dysart in 1925. His frame was like an ox with the strength of a lion, his heart was of melting gold, and from his voice came the thought and kindness of a saint.

Con's voice will always be remembered for his repertoire of songs, lifting his audience from the mud of the day's work to the celestial heights of romantic love. However many a drink he may have consumed, Con never failed to lift the heart of whoever he met, whether by song or a kind word.

It is not surprising the impression he made on those he met – from the President to the barman, Con Howard was the man in Dublin never to be forgotten. This may also be said of America, where he was for many years a Consul General in the Irish Embassy. He organised, with his life companion Mary Caulfield, a trip from Ireland to the states in honour of St. Brendan, discoverer of America.

20 of us set out on an excellent trip, efficiently organised by Con and Mary. I was surprised at how well Con was known in this vast continent by ordinary people as well as the President himself. I remember being proud to be taken into the House of Representatives by Con where he was recognised as if he was a member himself. And then to demonstrate his influence and make us proud of being a member of the Irish Embassy, he arranged for us all to have lunch at the White House, not with the President this time, but as I remember it well, we all ate at a round table. Such was the influence Con from the Co. Clare had in the White House.

Mixing with the most influential, especially the Irish-Americans, Con became good friends of the Kennedys and clicked with Jack. One evening at dinner Con persuaded Jack he would make it to the White House. This persuasion developed into influence and he became Jack's friend for life.

The day Neil Armstrong landed on the moon, all the scientists and politicians were present at a party and Con was there as a guest. Being a personality speaker, Con said, "This is a wonderful party, with such a large amount of people present. So the bill should be sent to the moon because it will be astronomical." This brought the house down!

Con Howard returned to Ireland from America and remained in the Foreign Office. He was disappointed not have become Ireland's Ambassador in Washington, and to compensate for this he was appointed by the Sri Lankan government as their Honorary Consul.

A person of influence and ever-abiding kindness, Con was always a friend to call on for help in any difficulty. To anyone in need he responded with complete enthusiasm and the humour that was a key part of his generous personality.

## PAT BYRNE
*In Memory of Con Howard*

Con filled the room, when he came in, with charm
And with *élan*. He was a man who came
From where the words you spoke bore weight and heft.
He left behind a presence felt, though gone.

He walked the world as if he owned it all.
He did, inside his head, and he knew well
That he could win the hearts of all he met
With his own wit, and with the ease of it.

He took life by the scruff, and gave his own:
No hurler on the ditch, he played his part
In Dublin, London or Ruan.
He hurled and won: Con was a team.

His lips held all the wit-lines of the years:
The ones he'd met had etched the crinkles round his face.
His smile was more than just a pose. It was
Himself, the man who filled the world with grace.

He would invite poets of the dispossessed to come
And read their verse at his at-ease soirées,
Invite them to black-pudding brunch and tea.
But most of all, he loved Brian Merriman,
Whose festival in Clare became his final hymn.

## MEMORIES OF CON HOWARD

A champion of the arts, of poetry,
He loved the spoken language, and the page,
He lived for words and knew the Iliad,
He knew the Aeneid and half of Heaney's work.
He was an inspiration and a sage.

# MARY CAULFIELD
Con And The United Arts Club

During the summer, Michael Lillis suggested I edit *Memories Of Con Howard*, so a group of Con's friends came together to remember and celebrate his life.

Con's patron saint Brendan may or may not have discovered America, but there is no doubt that Con opened up America to the Irish. He single-handedly opened the doors of the White House to successive Taoisigh to present the gift of shamrock to the US president on St. Patrick's Day.

US presidents were also well aware of Con's patron saint, for President Reagan referred to the Brendan Society in several of his speeches while in Ireland, and the Brendan Society were welcomed to lunches in the White House and to Christmas parties where we drank egg nog while a young African choir sang carols and President Reagan told jokes for 20 minutes. Dana Rohrabacher, the President's speechwriter, gave us a tour of the White House and showed us rooms closed to the other visitors.

But it wasn't just one-way traffic – for Con welcomed US presidential candidate Senator Eugene McCarthy to the United Arts Club where the ladies were thrilled to greet this great patrician figure and hear him read his aardvark poems. Con also organised a gala dinner in the club for another US presidential candidate, Senator George McGovern.

I would also like to mention something about Con's promotion of arts and culture with particular reference to the United Arts Club. At one stage the club was going through a valley period and was in great danger of closing down. Con found the money to keep it afloat, even digging into his pockets to make up the shortfall. Then to keep the club alive he filled it with journalists, judges, actors, ambassadors and captains of industry. It wasn't unusual to see Mr. Jefferson Smurfit and Dr. Barnes in deep conversation – perhaps making plans to extend their empires. He brought in the descendant of the last High King of Ireland – The O'Conor Don, who talked about the Raj and his time in India. Another famous visitor was Joseph Judge, executive editor of National Geographic magazine whose 'Plain Spoken Poems Of Alaska' Con published for the United Arts Club. And Mr. Judge and his entourage of 30 recited there to great acclaim.

Another of Con's guests at the club was the internationally-acclaimed Australian artist Sir Sidney Nolan. Con suggested to Sir Sidney that he might like to donate some of his paintings to the Irish Museum of Modern Art (IMMA). Sir Sidney agreed, and the paintings formed the nucleus of the museum's collection. Con made the same suggestion to David O'Doherty (Patrick Ireland) and he also donated paintings to IMMA.

The late Patricia Boylan, author of the history of the Arts Club (*All Cultivated People*) described in glowing terms Con's handling of the 75th anniversary of the United Arts Club – as a result of which Richard Kingston presented the beautiful seascape hanging in the hallway of the club. I remember during the celebration seeing functions on three levels in the club at the same time– Brendan Kennelly holding a poetry workshop on the first floor, John Banville reading from his latest novel in the basement and videos (on loan from National Geographic in America) being shown in the drawing room – and this when videos were unheard of in Ireland. Con chose to launch his Cumann Merriman in the club, and thereby introduce to Ireland the concept of the summer school.

Con followed the great German philosopher Friedrich Nietzsche's dictum that, "We should consider every day lost on which we have not danced at least once, and we should call every truth false that was not accompanied by at least one laugh." Only the Arts Club could provide a platform for such a philosophy, for it is a place where all branches of the arts are honoured with passion – where the very atmosphere is intoxicating and where it would be impossible to spend a forgettable evening.

Con was truly one of the "minds to whom our heights of race belong".

# BRENDAN CONWAY
A Hoary Old Celt

I know of nobody more worthy of a memoir than my late and loved fellow Clareman, Con Howard.

It is recognised that persons of greatness, or indeed persons destined to become great, radiate an aura which lingers in the atmosphere of the location where they perform their life tasks. There is a phrase which describes this phenomenon – 'psychic presence'.

I first became aware of the psychic presence of Con Howard in the mid-1940s, when those of us who enrolled at St. Flannan's College, Ennis, heard of the academic record of this recent past pupil of the school. The student was Con Howard, who, it was told and re-told, had taught himself Greek to Leaving Certificate standard, and had gained first place in Ireland in the subject, together with a battery of other subjects. At that stage we had never met Con the man, but the aura persisted.

Several years later our paths crossed in Dublin, where Con was progressing his glittering career in the Department of External Affairs. At a very early stage of our friendship it became clear to me that sedate bureaucracy was not the way of life chosen by Con for himself. Indeed he saw his role as affirming and broadcasting the glory of Irish culture to as wide an audience as he could reach.

I now know that this restless motivation derived from a deep-seated patriotic conviction that we Irish, by ancestry, by destiny and even by birthright, were the greatest race on earth. My God, wasn't he, to the end, willing to let the world know about us!

From a litany of the achievements of his career I identify just three major symbols on his crowded escutcheon:

Con Howard's name will be forever and appropriately linked with the founding of Cumann Merriman. It pleases me to recall that I responded to his invitation in May 1967 to attend a gathering at the United Arts Club, where, "We will be talking about Brian Merriman." The Feakle poet lies in the same graveyard where my ancestors and my parents are buried. Con knew that, and announced my role at that gathering as "a cultural descendant of Merriman."

One had to be impressed by the team of star-studded speakers on the night – Daithí Ó Huaithne, Patrick Henchy, Michael Ó hAodha, to mention but a few.

The evening was enlivened by the singing of Nioclás Tóibín, Cantóir Na Rinne, and his performance of 'Sliabh na mBan' readied us for new and challenging adventures. But the key business of the evening was to enlist support for the erection of a proper memorial to Brian Merriman.

That was the foundation gathering of Cumann Merriman, and the first Scoil Samhraidh of Cumann Merriman took place at Ennis in autumn 1968, and there's been an annual gathering every year since. At the risk of repeating the cliché – the rest is history. In retrospect, we saw in action that momentous evening the restless energy and spirit of the 'we can do' philosophy that was characteristic of Con throughout his life.

With Cumann Merriman bedded down as a thriving agent of cultural formation, Con perhaps relaxed for a few years and enjoyed the success story which then already was, and still is, Cumann Merriman. But 'at ease' was never an order his spirit obeyed. He knew that we Irish, at home and in diaspora, needed a wider and more challenging horizon for exploration.

In a moment of inspiration he responded to the dream-making

quality of Sean Davey's music of *The Brendan Voyage*, and so the Brendan Society came into existence. I can recall his answer to my innocent query as to the relevance of St. Brendan to the programme of the St. Brendan Society. He replied, "St. Brendan epitomised the permanent struggle of man with nature, and points the road of success to Irish people of all ages."

I still meditate on that reply.

One morning in 1982/3 I took Con's telephone call to learn that his next project was an international conference to celebrate the bicentenary of Australia as a nation. He had already decided the conference would take place in Kilkenny Castle, would be launched by President Hillery and told me "you are the chairman of the local organising committee".

It all happened too! In autumn 1983 many Australian academics came, saw and were conquered by the exuberance of Con, and the Kilkenny conference gave rise to the publication of several important reference books of Australian history.

There are many other epiphanies through which one can but admire Con's achievements as diplomat, networker, innovator and job maker. Of course he can be described as a bon viveur, a raconteur, a songster (willing, but awful!) and an unrepentant Clareman. But, in my opinion, none of the above encapsulates the Con we all loved as fully as the description of him by professor Kevin B. Nowlan, who, in an off-the-cuff remark, coined the immortal comment: "Con is indeed a hoary old Celt."

He was all of that indeed. "Leaba i measc na n-aingeal go raibh aige".

# ANTHONY CRONIN
Structures Of Lasting Value Sprang From The Ground He Trod

Con Howard reminded me of the great Russian general, Katusov, as described by Tolstoy in *War And Peace*. On the day before a battle in which all could be won or lost everything was chaos and confusion. Katusov seemed unable to grasp the situation and worse still to care whether he did or not. Before the Battle of Borodino his seeming indifference to the outcome is such that he falls asleep in the sun. When battle is joined Katusov is seen to be the great master, with every thread in his hands and every contingency foreseen.

When Con was in the Embassy in Washington sometime in the '70s, I went there to lecture at the Smithsonian. I was to stay for four days and Con announced that we were going to give a reading in the Embassy on the third of them. I protested. Where were the readers? Where was the audience? It proved to be an exceptionally happy and successful event. William Meredith, then poet librarian of Congress, wrote to me afterwards to say that there were many readings about which more notice had been given but never one so genial.

And besides being an organiser of mysterious powers and abilities, Con was also what is nowadays called a facilitator and one with an exceptionally lucky touch. I had been describing to him the resolution of the Wood Quay situation and expressing the hope that it would never recur. The following night he brought the archaeologists Michael Herity and Brendan O'Riordan round to his house. They described how the Danish city extended far beyond Wood Quay and drew a map which included a large section of Temple Bar. This, they said, could not be excavated then, because there simply weren't the resources. Low-rise development was the answer, they explained. It was high-rise that did the damage. Low-rise would be like a Chubb lock and would keep what was there safe. When I got back to Dublin I showed the archaeologists' map to the Taoiseach Charlie Haughey and at that point the idea of Temple Bar as a cultural quarter was born. There was a long way to go. Much of it had to be wrested from CIE, who then owned most of it, and structures had to be set up but this was the beginning of what has turned out to be the Temple Bar we now know.

If the task of a diplomat is, as I suppose, to get people on the side of a country you represent, Con did the job superbly. He charmed and interested people to such an extent and was at the same time so patently Irish that many who did not know otherwise assumed that Ireland must be an exceptionally charming and interesting place. Structures of lasting value such as the Ireland-Australia Society seemed to spring from the ground he trod. And it was he who almost single-handedly invented the concept of what we now call the Diaspora. It was certainly through him that people such as the painters Sidney Nolan and Arthur Boyd became more deeply conscious of the ties, whether mythological or otherwise, that bound them to their ancestral country.

There used to be two cultural streams in Ireland. One, which often disappointed in the end, was what might be called the Belvedere-Bar Library tradition. The other was that which I liked to regard as descended from the Hedge School and which knew what it knew so well and held it so dear that it often recited it in the pub and sang it if it could. Con could not sing, though he often produced a version of singing which like, I am told, some Himalayan singing was all on one note. Unfortunately most of his career was passed at a time when the civil service was governed by what Richard Kempinski in *The Emperor* has called 'the negative knowledge'. If you knew what not to do and sedulously abided by your knowledge you were safe.

It was activity which got you into trouble. Con's aberrations – and there is no doubt that he was by times aberrant – bulked larger in certain official minds than his achievements. He made that matter very little. I don't think I ever heard him use the word 'culture' but he was passionate about cultural things. And he was, wherever he went, and whatever his official position, a superlative cultural ambassador.

## SEÁN DONLON
A True Patriot

Con and I were colleagues in the Department of Foreign Affairs for a quarter of a century. I first encountered him in the Gresham Hotel in Dublin in June 1963 where he had set up a Press Centre for the journalists who were in Ireland to cover the visit of President John F. Kennedy. He seemed to know them all, Irish, American, British and whatever. He introduced me to the first Japanese person I ever met and asked me to mind him, as he was not used to the volume of alcohol Irish and American journalists could drink!

Con's energetic, creative and selfless approach to his job was what struck me in 1963, and continued to impress me for the rest of his career. He served as Consul General in Boston, as Press Officer in the Embassy in London and as Press Counsellor in the Embassy in Washington DC. In between, he held positions in the Department's headquarters in Dublin. Somehow he also embraced a very wide range of extra-curricular activities, including (but not limited to) Cumann Merriman, the British-Irish Association, the St. Brendan Society, the Irish-Australian Society and the United Arts Club. It was at the Arts Club that, on the occasion of his departure to Washington, Charles J. Haughey presented him with a portrait and described him as a national treasure.

It is difficult, in a short piece, to cover even a small part of Con's life. There is no doubt, however, that one of his finest professional chapters was his term as Press Officer in London. He was there when the Northern Ireland troubles started in 1969, and he was the face of Ireland in Britain during the following difficult years. He was widely known on Fleet Street and in the Palace of Westminster, and did much to keep open the channels of communication between

Dublin and London during an era that included Bloody Sunday, the introduction of internment in Northern Ireland, the first murders of British soldiers, and the planting of bombs in Britain by the Provisional IRA.

During the London posting, his unique approach was evident in him bringing a group of British journalists to Dublin for briefings by Government Ministers, and then hiring a train to bring them to a Munster hurling final in Thurles. Such was the hospitality on board the train, and in Thurles, that they returned to Dublin over a day behind schedule – much to the distress of CIE, as the company had other demands for their train on a busy Monday morning.

In many ways, Con was most at home in the US – he had lengthy postings in Boston and Washington DC – where the warmth of his personality and his encyclopaedic knowledge of Ireland captured the widest range of contacts any Irish diplomat has ever had. His friends included the Kennedys, Tip O'Neill, Cardinals, Governors and Mayors. But he also held court in Irish pubs in Boston, Washington and New York, and used his position and contacts to solve hundreds of passport, visa and related problems. It was typical of his approach that when an undocumented and uninsured Irish student was seriously injured in an accident, Con arranged free first-class hospitalization, and when the student died a few weeks later Con persuaded a Boston undertaker to transport the remains to Ireland without charge. His helpfulness even extended to rescuing a dog, Michelle, whom he eventually brought back to Ireland, boarding her in expensive quarantine in Dublin for the requisite three months.

Con's funeral Mass and burial in his native Dysart in County Clare was an appropriate tribute. It included the best of local traditional music, great conversation, good drink and food and, for many, a very late night. The range of people in Dysart that day, including family, friends, locals, academics, colleagues, clergy and journalists, said it all. Con's friendships and influence extended far and wide, and his energy and talents served Ireland well. He was a true patriot.

# JAMES DOWNEY
An extract from *In My Own Time*

Con Howard was press counsellor at the Irish embassy in London. He had a rare genius for making contacts – and for turning them into close friends. One was the future Chancellor of the Exchequer Denis Healey, who had possibly the finest intellect in the British Labour Party. Howard would go on to make similarly impressive contacts in Washington. In the early 1970s he addressed himself to a quixotic effort to convert the Conservative Party to the Irish nationalist cause. He reported to Iveagh House on a conversation with Lady Hartwell, daughter of Lord Birkenhead and wife of Lord Hartwell, proprietor of the *Telegraph*. She was considered a person of enormous influence. She asked him if we really wanted to take on board "those screaming women in the Shankill Road". A pertinent question.

## DESMOND FENNELL
Filled With Ireland

It was around the time that he was preaching the gospel of St. Brendan the Navigator in the USA that I had most contact with Con. He had me and others investigating the location and time of the Viking bridgehead in North America and, simultaneously, studying Brendan's imram, written much before that, to identify the route that the Irish saint and his companions took across the North Atlantic. The point was to identify which part of North America – the Bahamas? New England? – the Irish navigator reached, and to declare him the real discoverer of America.

With the news that St. Brendan was indeed that, I accompanied Con to lovely Annapolis and to the founding of the American Society of St. Brendan with an American naval officer as its President. But having only one string to his bow on a visit to the USA, or indeed anywhere, was never Con's style. So I recall, after Annapolis, ascending the steps of the Capitol in Washington with him and entering its hallowed hall. His purpose was to attend a festive gathering of those Representatives and Senators who belonged to the Irish-American caucus of Congress that he had founded some years previously. Indeed, I think that the point of the festive gathering was to celebrate the pre-announced visit of their founder and animator. The final act of that 'business trip' was a visit to the New York apartment of the art critic Brian O'Doherty (the painter, Patrick Ireland) to discuss the how and when of his presentation of a collection of paintings to the Irish Museum of Modern Art in Dublin. To speak of Con's vitality is to be banal. For myself, I remember it particularly in two respects: in the mornings after a late, hard-drinking night when it was obvious from his rapid-fire speech that his brain had spent the night meticulously ordering the next day's activities; that, and his rapid strides as he moved from one appointment to the next. From our American visit I recall how it was that everywhere we went he was well known and remembered from previous enjoyable encounters, welcomes evident in the smiling faces that greeted him. He was a good listener too, his concentration on what was being said to him showing in the obvious ticking of his mind as he registered, sifted, and stored for future action.

  Overall, and movingly, I recall him as filled with Ireland, and its standing and interests in the world; a man of whom to use the word 'patriot' is to understate.

## SEAMUS HEANEY
*The Disappearing Island*

Once we presumed to found ourselves for good
Between its blue hills and those sandless shores
Where we spend our desperate night in prayer and vigil,

Once we had gathered driftwood, made a hearth
And hung our cauldron like a firmament,
The island broke beneath us like a wave.

The land sustaining us seemed to hold firm
Only when we embraced it *in extremis*.
All I believe that happened there was vision.

\* This poem was first read at a dinner for Tim Severin, organised by Con and the Brendan Society. Seamus Heaney suggested the following quotation could be said of Con: "Every year on the anniversary of his death the nation should declare two minutes of pandemonium."

# MONICA HENCHY
## A Faithful Visitor

My late husband, Patrick Henchy, could claim to have known Con Howard longer than most of his friends. He knew Con growing up in Dysart in Corofin, Co. Clare, and later taught him in the Christian Brothers School in Ennis. He remembered Con cycling every day into Ennis on a battered bike, with his school bag precariously clipped on to his carrier as he pounded the dusty road. His copybooks were often damp and mud-splattered, but when Paddy opened them to read an essay that had to be deciphered through an untidy scrawl, he recognised the outpourings of an original mind.

When Con was appointed a Clerical Officer in the Department of Industry and Commerce some years later he came to Dublin and contacted Paddy. He explained that he was thinking of doing the Third Secretaries exam for the Department of Foreign Affairs, but as his Irish had become rather rusty (Irish, as Con wryly commented, being very important should you be posted to Africa!) he asked Paddy to give him a grind. Paddy was happy to comply, as he enjoyed the repartee that would ensue in both languages.

As founder of Cumann Merriman, Con worked tirelessly to promote it. It was Con's idea to publish *America and Ireland 1776-1976* – the proceedings of the successful Cumann Merriman Bicentennial Conference in Ennis in August, 1976. Con was based in Washington and there were regular phone calls to our house from Con at 2am (much to the discomfort of our family) and then, at Con's instigation, from Owen Dudley Edwards and David Doyle, the joint editors, at 8am seeking information on the progress of the volume, as Paddy had the unenviable task of acting as a go-between.

It was Con's idea, too, to organise a visit to the US for members of Cumann Merriman to publicise the book, and Con arranged for us to meet Edward Kennedy and the Speaker, John McCormack, in the House of Representatives. Then followed another whistle-stop ride to Boston where Con had persuaded Fr. McFadden, President of Stonehill College, to put on a banquet for us with Irish music and witty speeches. Here, by a coincidence, we discovered that the gentleman who promoted the banquet was the same person who had been fishing with Paddy on Lake Inchiquin in Corofin the year before – a fact which greatly facilitated the smooth operation of the event.

There were times when Con, because of his enthusiastic ventures and persuasive energy, could be exasperating, but he never forgot Paddy's help and encouragement, and was a faithful visitor while Paddy was in hospital, regaling him with amusing anecdotes of Dublin's social life. This colourful character was definitely "sui generis". *Is fíor nach mbeidh a leithéid ann arís.*

# NUALA HOGAN
## A Wicked Sense Of Humour

In the spring of 1977 a development association was set up in Feakle parish with the object of bringing some employment and life to the area. The job of promoting the lakes had begun, and interest was being shown by some British coarse angling clubs.

On a Sunday morning in May, Con Howard breezed onto the scene with the late Birdie Cunningham, Honorary Secretary, to meet Jack Hogan, Chairman. Con's idea was to revive interest in a suitable memorial to the famous poet Brian Merriman. This had been mooted in 1947 and 1948 with Eamon de Valera as a patron. But some locals had objected to the bawdy content of the poem, and the matter had been allowed to drop. But after attitudes had softened, the project was taken on again and with enthusiasm. With Con as the driving force and using his considerable powers of persuasion, swift progress was made. To raise funds, a sports day was held in the village, with members of the Riordans tv programme as the star attractions, arranged, of course, by Con. If anything went wrong St. Jude got a rest – you just rang Con, and problem solved! The crowds were enormous, as Tom, Minnie and Benjy from The Riordans were real celebrities. They judged the children's Fancy Dress and officiated at the Donkey Derby, and Tom auctioned stuff from the jumble stall – all very innocent – and the Riordans gave their services free, also, of course, arranged by Con.

In September, Con arranged two very successful concerts in Liberty Hall in Dublin on the eves of the All-Ireland Hurling and Football finals. At that time he established a small group of his friends in high places (of which he had many) to help. This group was later to be known as Cumann Merriman.

The plaque was unveiled in July '68 by the late Dr. Hillery and the famous poem was read by the equally famous Siobhân McKenna. The day itself was another huge success. All sectors were represented – Church and State intellectuals, musicians and the common people. Con was a remarkable organiser, but he never hogged the limelight, but was always there when needed. He was solely responsible for the founding of Cumann Merriman, and it is due to his vision that it is now the success it is. In short – No Con – No plaque – No Cumann Merriman.

He was a man of high intellect, combined with a wicked sense of humour, and who treated rich and poor alike. He gave 100% to any undertaking he was interested in, and had the happy knack of motivating others – a very special man indeed. As they say in Clare he had 'the coaxyorum (charisma) in full measure'. We miss you Con, God rest you.

# CATHERINE JENNINGS
Travels With Con And The Brendan Society

In Irish history we come across references to the contact historic personages had with places abroad… St. Colmcille and Iona, the Wild Geese and France, and St. Brendan and the tradition of St. Borondan in the Canary Islands. What was extraordinary about Con is that the Brendan Society which he founded turned what was the stuff of legend into reality and so, we ended up in Iona, or in Bordeaux, or in Spain, in the steps of Irish saints, scholars or soldiers. When the bicentennial of the French Revolution was approaching, Con set about organising a trip that would encompass many periods of contact between Ireland and France, from the age of St. Columbanus onwards to the 20$^{th}$ century. For some reason I thought a tour of Brittany would be the appropriate start to a tour ending in Paris. However, Con consulted Jean-Michel Picard of UCD and over dinner in the Arts Club the less obvious choice of a tour northwards of Paris was conceived and agreed on. Jean-Michel pointed out that in the seventh and eighth centuries, Irish monks travelling to the Continent would have avoided long sea voyages. They would have gone first to Britain, and then crossed to what is now France and Belgium, penetrating into those regions along the rivers Seine, Marne and Somme. It was a revelation to find that many towns in Northern France and Southern Belgium are proud to claim their origins in Irish monastic foundations established by monks whose names are no longer familiar to us – Saints Fursey and Faolan (aka Feuillen or Pholien) – and to discover the many offshoots of Columbanus' establishments in eastern France.

As was usual for the Brendan Society, the itinerary widened as preparations got under way, and the 1989 trip ended up including a visit to the Irish College in Paris, another to the extensive military graveyards of World War I, and to the major parades in Paris for the commemoration of the Revolution. Jean-Michel Picard organised a wonderful panel of French and Irish historians who spoke to us in Paris. Attending the parades on July 14 was not easy, as many centre-city Metro stations shut down, and some of us gave up the struggle to attend the events and returned to our hotel to watch them on television! We also got to the Irish College for the launch of the book *The Green Cockade* by Fr. Liam Swords.

We attended mass in an old Benedictine monastery of St. Wandrille, not far from Rouen, and one of the monks gave us a guided tour of the establishment. We were surprised to learn that this ancient French monastery initially followed the rule of St. Columbanus. In the Library of Laon, close to the Belgian border, we were shown a manuscript of the Latin version of the Navigatio Sancti Brendani from the monastery of Vauclair. If I remember correctly, it was dated from the 14$^{th}$ century. In the church of St. John the Baptist in Peronne we saw a stained glass window which described how the choice of a burial place for St. Fursey was made. Several towns wished to hold his remains as he was famed for having had an intense vision of Hell, so his sanctity was thereby guaranteed, and any town having his relics would become a centre of pilgrimage. The solution was to place Fursey's body on a cart drawn by oxen to a crossroads, and, in the presence of all the local clerical and civil authorities, allow the oxen to choose the direction of the destination of the holy man's bones. Peronne thus became Fursey's final destination.

Jean-Michel Picard edited the lectures given at the end of this trip in a book, *Ireland And Northern France,* published by the Four Courts Press in 1991. It was launched in the National Museum in

Dublin by Máire Geoghegan-Quinn TD, then Junior Minister for European Affairs, with the French ambassador to Ireland in attendance.

Máire Geoghegan-Quinn spoke glowingly of Con's presence at talks preparatory to the Anglo-Irish agreement, describing how his good nature helped ease many fraught moments during negotiations.

In Ireland over the years the Brendan Society had meetings in Galway, Ballyferriter and Clonfert, exploring various aspects of the Brendan legend. One trip was intended to the island of Inis Gloire off Blacksod in Co. Mayo, because it had traditional links with St. Brendan and is also associated with the legend of the Children of Lir, banished there for 300 years. However, a trip to Inis Gloire proved difficult to arrange, as the uninhabited island had no proper pier or slipway, and a visit would have to take into consideration the tides and wind direction to enable boats make safe landfall.

Another entertaining trip was to the Bordeaux region in France. Historically, France must have been the source of wine imported into Ireland for the celebration of the mass. The wine trade grew over the centuries in Bordeaux and many English and Irish traders went into business and settled there. Wines from Bordeaux are found with names of vineyards owned by Irish proprietors: Chateaux Clarke, Phelan, McCarthy, Talbot, Kirwan, and Lynch-Bages among many others. We contacted Anthony Barton (Barton et Guestier) of Chateau Langoa, and were delighted with his prompt response and kind invitation to call. He informed us he would be abroad at the time of our visit, but he delegated the duty of entertaining us to his daughter Lilianne. We had a very pleasant tour of the Chateau Langoa vineyard, followed by a tasting of their prestigious wines in the care of a wonderful hostess.

Moving into distilled wines, we contacted the Hennessy distillery in Cognac and were again met with great hospitality by that family of Irish descent. Mr. Killian Hennessy (since deceased) wrote to say he would ask Maurice Hennessy to show us round their business, which he duly did. The tall, genial and handsome Maurice looked as if he had left Co. Cork only yesterday, and he introduced us to a new line in their brandy production, 'Pure White', which the company hoped would attract a younger age group to the traditional spirit.

When it came to contraband and smuggling in Ireland in the 18th and 19th centuries, brandy was the most prized drink for the Irish, as can be deduced from so many remote piers in counties Galway or Kerry being named 'Brandy Harbour'. And it seems that the 'fion Spainneach' mentioned in poems such as 'Roisin Dubh' referred to brandy, not wine.

Another interesting trip in Con's company was to Hungary where we visited the famed picture of Our Lady of Gyor in its magnificent shrine in the city of Gyor, regarded as miraculous by devout Catholics there. The painting was left there by a 17th century Bishop of Clonfert, Walter Lynch, who had to flee Ireland following the Cromwellian invasion and subsequent persecution, and was given refuge in the Cathedral of Gyor by the local bishop. After he died in exile a painting of the Madonna, which had been in his possession, was seen to shed tears of blood. The linen used to collect the tears is reserved as a venerated relic in Gyor cathedral. Every year, on St. Patrick's Day, the present Bishop of Gyor holds a commemorative High Mass in memory of the Irish refugee bishop of Clonfert Walter Lynch who found sanctuary in Hungary. A replica of the painting was recently gifted to Loughrea Cathedral by the Hungarian Government and presented to Bishop John Kirby by the Bishop of Gyor. During our visit to Budapest we were given every help by the

First Secretary in the Irish embassy there, and were invited to the Embassy's traditional reception for St. Patrick's Day. In the group at that time was the late Nuala Boland who said she thoroughly enjoyed the trip.

One far-flung expedition for the Brendan Society was to Mexico to investigate the San Patricio Brigade's sacrifices during Mexico's resistance to US invasion and occupation.

Another trip to Argentina involved the Brendan society, but Con was not in the small group that eventually travelled. Rose Rushe of Limerick, Joe and Angela Kelly of Galway, and the witty and erudite broadcaster John Quinn all participated in that trip. Many of the Society's members who usually travelled abroad for St. Patrick's Day were concerned by the length of the flight to Buenos Aires (our aging profile no doubt a factor), and the possibility of deep vein thrombosis was mentioned, and these concerns must have deterred potential participants. When we returned after a marvellous trip the reaction in the Arts Club was "why weren't we told about this?" One of the high points was a visit to the National Basilica of Our Lady of Lujan where a side altar was dedicated to the Irish community and dominated by a stained glass window depicting St. Patrick in all his glory. A plaque informed us that a pilgrimage of 9,000 Irish people had been there in 1901 in the company of the Archbishop of Buenos Aires to celebrate the start of the new century.

What should not be forgotten is the focus Con brought at home in Ireland to historic links between this country and the USA and Australia. In 1976 the Merriman Summer School hosted a bicentennial conference in Ennis on 'The American Identity and the Irish Connection', the proceedings of which were published. Later, circa 1990, Con presided over a memorable conference in Galway at which members of the Durack family spoke. Writer Mary Durack left an account of the family settling into life in Western Australia in her book *Kings In Grass Castles*, and artist Elizabeth Durack exhibited some of her paintings. A brother spoke of the pioneering days for the Durack family in Western Australia, an experience as adventurous and as dangerous as anything to come from the American Wild West. In addition, the conference was honoured by the presence of Australian artist, Sir Sidney Nolan.

Iona, Annaghdown on Lough Corrib in Co. Galway and Clonfert Cathedral are present in the Brendan legend, and visiting all of those places of significance in Irish history with Con has enriched our lives. *Bheadh Con molta agus mise i mo thost… as an méid a rinne sé ar mhaithe le cultúr, cursaí léinn agus stáir na hÉireann. Go gcuití Dia dhuit é, a Chon.*

Thanks for the memories, Con.

HAIKU FOR CON HOWARD

Iarthar an Chláir -
comhdháil rúnda
na ndéithe dearmadta

West Clare -
secret convention
of forgotten gods

IMAGE: RON ROSENSTOCK  TEXT: GABRIEL ROSENSTOCK

Above: Con in Berlin;
(right) with Anne Mac Donagh;
with the poet Maria Mooney
in Washington; Opposite page:
Con with his dog, Michelle.

Clockwise from top: Con with Ambassador Wickremesuige – Sri Lankan Ambassador to Great Britain and his wife, Mary Caulfield and Sri Lankan First Secretary Chitrangawewagaswara and her husband; Con at the San Patricio plaque; portrait of Con by Mick O'Dea.

*The Wild Geese* series, presented by Sir Sidney Nolan to IMMA at Con's behest.

Clockwise from top: Con with Proinsias Mac Aonghusa (photo by John Horgan, courtesy of Clare County Library); with his daughter Aileen in California; with Anne Mac Donagh, Mary O'Donnell, Eithne Manley and Cyril Cusack; at Monte Alban, Mexico, with Mary Caulfield, Hugh Hehir, Julie Caulfield and Gabrielle Allman.

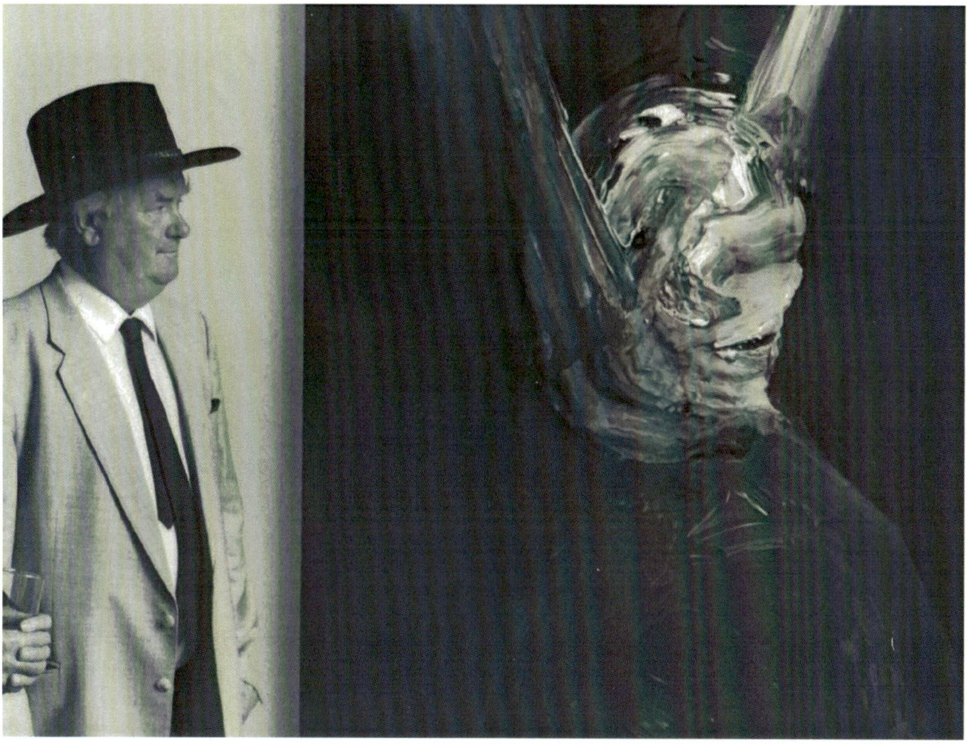

Clockwise from top: Con with a Sidney Nolan painting at the Australia-Ireland conference; Con, John Ryan, Bob Ryan, Owen Mac Donagh and Essie Harrington at the steps of the House of Representatives, Washington; with Anne Mac Donagh, Joseph Judge (executive editor of *National Geographic*) and Phyllis Judge; with Sir Sidney and Lady Nolan.

Harry Clarke's *The Brendan Window* in Tullamore, Co. Offaly and (below) Con at a Byron Society salon with Monica Henchy and founder Mary Caulfield.

# JOSEPH JUDGE
Letter To Con Howard

*Joseph Judge organised an Irish holiday for his close friends and their children, for the purpose of informing the young people about their Irish heritage and roots. There were 32 persons involved. They hired nine cars and went around Ireland for two weeks. Mr. Judge gave them at least 100 lectures on Irish history, culture and the Irish-American connection. The following letter to Con Howard describes their Irish experience.*

Dear Con:

The 32 Potomac Irish are safely returned from their most glorious trip to Ireland, with nary a whimper, complaint, or hard word the entire time among the lot of them – only the certain knowledge they were having the trip of a lifetime and that strange emotion of opening in their lives a new but familiar chapter. It was entirely and completely and wholly wonderful, every day of it, and when we all gathered to celebrate the 'Glorious Fourth' in Mac McGarry's great backyard, we did our traditional readings of patriotic literature – Jefferson's second Inaugural and the like – and I read a piece about Rufus King refusing the 1798 men visas to America, and Ginny Keefe read a selection from Mary Antin about the Boston ghetto.

I owe you a special and particular thanks for arranging the reading at the Arts Club and for that extraordinary lunch at the Grey Door – and the tickets to the reception at Dublin Castle. I must admit right out that to hear my poems read so beautifully in that setting was one of the shining hours of my life, and the fact they were well received by the audience and Ulick O'Connor made the satisfaction of the moment complete – and allayed my fears that you might have been embarrassed if we had laid an egg. In fact, the poetry was sound. The readings were nothing short of superb, and we will all remember it for a very, very long time.

I assume that the poems were picked up from the Iona House and arrived safely in your possession and will be making their way home across the Atlantic.

Next, I must thank you for Desmond Fennell and Maweenish – for me, the finest moment of the trip, because of the place and the man. We sat up until God knows when, drinking that Irish moonshine and talking about life and poetry and conscience – the kind of evening that in my life never happens anymore, or so seldom it is to be cherished. Desmond is an authentic person, as you know better than I, and his son Ossian a splendid young man whom we all loved at once.

The four families left in old Garrywadreen rolled out the carpet, and their own collection of moonshine (so when I got to Desmond's, I was already inured to the stuff; they had made a gift bottle for me and explained when I left they couldn't give it to me because I had drank it, and every other bottle in the village as well!) I suppose that was in character, as old James Judge had drunk out the farm in 1913, selling it off for 700 pounds – worth thousands, they said, thousands. The family that bought those Judge lands is still there and directed me to 93 year-old Michael Marley, in the old man's home in Castlebar, whom I talked to on a day of pouring down rain. I brought him a bottle of whiskey and he said: "Francis Judge reared a bad son when he reared James".

Went to Thoor Ballylee, and my son Michael recited Yeats' poetry the entire time. He knows by heart every line. Then to Newpark House near Ennis where Mr. Barron said he had been a classmate of yours – Corny, we called him. Your name came up as I was reciting the kindnesses of the people of Ireland toward our wandering group of distant cousins. I am afraid I may have offended Mr. Barron when I told him that less attention to the ancient wrongs of Ulster and more attention to the economic troubles of the Republic might serve Ireland better at the moment: he would have none of it. With his and his father's history, who would? They don't need a damned Yank lecturing them, but this is a Yank who carried stretchers in Korea and whose sons missed Vietnam by an eyelash and who knows that too much righting of ancient wrongs makes punks in Dublin.

In short, Con, you have my many thanks for many kind acts and deeds that helped to make our trip a special event in the lives of the people who lived it. History, after all, has to be a living history, and the Ireland of the American sentimental passed-down grandfather's version, though a rich and powerful thing, passed by in time a long time ago. I hope that the young people who came with us understand that Ireland has to live in the present, make its way as a nation, and provide for its people.

I have a feeling that in the fullness of time, the world is going to get out of control, and there will be the Irish antidote – at least in Garrywadreen, a little moonshine, a lot of rain, and a lot of love. God keep you.

Joe

First published as the concluding 'chapter' in *Plain Spoken Poems Of Alaska*, which was published by the United Arts Club.

## MORGAN LLYWELYN
A Complex Individual

A few rare individuals possess an extraordinary gift for friendship. Con Howard was one of those people. If he liked you, he loved you, and that love was unconditional. Con was unfailingly supportive of his friends. His knowledge of them was encyclopedic. He could recall more facts about them than they remembered themselves.

In 1981, Cornelius Howard was introduced to me in Washington DC, where he was the Irish Cultural Attaché. My second historical novel had just become an international bestseller and been highly praised by President Reagan. As a result I was thrust unprepared into the Washington scene. Con promptly took me under his wing. We had a lot in common, including the fact that we both were Irish Republicans at heart and our people came from Co. Clare. In the way such things happen among the Irish, we discovered that we were distantly related. Of course.

Con already had read *Lion Of Ireland: The Legend Of Brian Boru*, and could quote long passages from it. At the time I did not realise I was in the presence of a living legend, but I soon learned. Con knew everyone who mattered. Caught out by the unexpectedly huge success of 'Lion', my publishers had failed to mount an adequate publicity campaign for the book. Con took over. Within a matter of days I was on national television and heavily in demand for public appearances. A formerly unknown Irish king became the toast of America. Invitations from the great and the good were pouring in.

1981 passed in a breathtaking whirl of speeches and book tours and flash bulbs and White House lunches and diplomatic dinners. There was no time to savour 'being famous'. It seemed to happen magically, but much of the credit goes to Con. He was always in the background with a twinkle in his eye, telling more people about my writing. Con did not believe in faint praise but in glowing hyperbole. Modest to a fault about himself, he was an extravagant champion of others.

When the excitement died down a bit my husband Charles and I moved to New Hampshire. We did not see Con as often, but the telephone might ring at any moment with insider news of Ireland, a research suggestion for my next book, or an anecdote he thought we would enjoy. Then my husband was diagnosed with prostate cancer. Con recruited the unofficial Irish militia to support us with offers of anything we might need. President Reagan himself telephoned Charlie every few weeks to cheer him up.

Charlie died in March of 1985. Con was back in Ireland by then, and he arranged for the orchestra to play 'The Minstrel Boy' in Charlie's honour in the National Concert Hall. I moved home to Ireland that November. Home for good. Con Howard and Maureen O'Hara met me at Shannon Airport with a dozen red roses and a bottle of Jameson.

My furniture, personal belongings and countless books were shipped in a 40-foot container, which was then held up in Dublin Port for six weeks. No one in charge seemed to know where it was located or when it could be released. Meanwhile I slept on the floor of my rented house in Killaloe, under a pile of coats. One morning I happened to mention this while talking to Con on the phone. He said only, "I'll see what I can do." The container was delivered to my door that same evening, together with a very polite customs inspector who personally drove out from Limerick to get everything released to

me. Alerted by Con, the inspector brought his own copy of 'Lion' to be autographed.

Con never did anything by halves. An invitation from him could involve a black-tie gala or an uproarious seisún in a highly disreputable pub. When my son Seán was taking a law course in Trinity, Con invited him for breakfast. As Seán later related, "I had a breakfast with Con Howard that lasted until the next morning." It remains one of his most treasured memories.

Researching historical fiction requires a lot of travel. In the most unlikely foreign capitals I have been regaled with colourful Con Howard stories. He was famous both for his cultural knowledge and for his larger than life personality. No-one who met him forgot him. After retirement, Con refused to slow down. His health was not always good but his spirit remained robust. He undertook one project after another with his usual irresistible enthusiasm, promoting Irish artists and encouraging interest in Irish history and archeology. Yet he always found time for his friends, whom he relentlessly recruited to his many causes.

The years took their toll on Con as they do on all of us, but he did not go gentle into that good night. He remained himself to the end. Tough and tender, fighter and lover, brilliant and mad, a poet and a peasant and a king. The last time I spoke with him, shortly before he died, he was still making plans. In his mind they all came to fruition, those exciting projects of his. Ireland is richer for them.

The *Oxford English Dictionary* defines 'complex' as "consisting of many different and connected parts; not easy to analyse or understand; complicated or intricate" and "having both a real and imaginary part". By any definition, Con Howard was a complex individual. Each person who knew him knew a different man. He lived in the real world, but also in a more brightly coloured sphere where the banners were always flying and the music was always playing.

If I ever reach the Pearly Gates I expect to find Con Howard just inside, with a twinkle in his eye, eager to introduce me to everyone who matters.

# BRENDAN LYNCH
## A Man Of Myriad Enthusiasms

"God bless Con Howard and all his enthusiasms! He brought us culture – and long overdue fun," enthused a back-seat passenger in one of my books.

Professor Jimmy O'Donovan was on his merry way back to Lisdoonvarna after a dance in Fanore.

It was only four o'clock in the afternoon. The Atlantic gleamed in the sun.

"Merriman would have been proud of him, he was a Renaissance man," Jimmy thumped his chauffeur's back. Their car lurched towards the last stonewall between them and the New World.

Con bestrode those two worlds like a Colossus. A diplomat in Boston, he became a friend of President John F. Kennedy. Some of Con's overseas amorous and drinking escapades almost caused diplomatic incidents. But the gregarious Dysart man did more to publicise and popularise Ireland than a host of better-behaved ambassadors. Tip O'Neill, Speaker of the US House of Representatives, observed: "If Con Howard and I stood for Mayor of Boston tomorrow, Con would win."

The Clareman also became a friend of British Prime Minister Ted Heath after founding the British-Irish Associations. His Irish-Australia Association led to Sidney Nolan's gift of valuable paintings to Ireland. The St. Brendan Society was another inspired brainchild. This man of a myriad enthusiasms was also a consistent supporter of lesser-known artists and writers.

With the late Muriel Allison, Con is one of the dedicatees of my new book, *Prodigals And Geniuses. The Writers And Artists Of Dublin's Baggotonia.* Peadar MacManus, a fellow member of the United Arts Club, sums him up well in that book: "With his scholarship, wit and zest for life, Con Howard could make Socrates smile over breakfast, best Cicero at a discursive lunch, and see Dionysus to bed after a long evening." ere was only one Con Howard.

## PEADAR MAC MÁGHNAIS
The Spirit Of Merriman

*"Más maith olc í nó donaí mar iarracht*
*Is geal liom i thionscnamh i dtosach don fhialfhear*
*Con Howard a chur Cumann*
*Merriman ar bun agus*
*A bhronn ar dhroma eile obair a riartha."*

This teasing compliment, paid by Gearóid Ó Clérigh to his professional colleague, explains the essence of Con Howard's relationship with Cumann Merriman. Con was the *only begetter* of the Cumann, and was happy to pass on the administration to those who were attracted to the idea. An effort had been made to erect a memorial plaque in Feakle to Brian Merriman by a group that included Cearbhall Ó Dálaigh and Richard Ellmann in 1946. It did not succeed because of local opposition. However, the idea persisted and Con founded Cumann Merriman in 1967. The immediate objectives were the erection of the plaque, and the publication of a new edition of *Cúirt An Mhean Oíche*. The plaque was designed by Seamus Murphy and was unveiled with local approval following Con's diplomatic work in Co. Clare. The perception of Merriman as the author of "a dirty poem" had changed to that of a major literary figure who, as Yeats observed in 1926, might have founded a modern Gaelic literature, had political circumstances been different. The new edition of the poem, edited by David Greene, was published by Dolmen Press in 1968. Eamon de Valera agreed to be Patron of the Cumann.

Con's next big idea was to have a Merriman Summer School in Ennis. The Yeats School had been a great success in Sligo, and attracted Yeatsian scholars from all over the world. The Merriman School was conceived as having more of a fun element, while maintaining serious academic standards. There would be an emphasis on bilingualism. The old constraints were loosening. John Montague declared that puritan Ireland was dead and gone after the Mullingar Fleadh. Con was determined to put this to the test. He succeeded in attracting an extraordinarily talented group of people to help in organising the School. People like Donal Foley and Ciarán Mac Mathúna were invaluable for publicity. The School was held in September 1968 and was a huge success. The John Horgan collection of photographs taken at the School, now in the Clare County Library, shows the wide range of people present. The diversity of the talent was a reflection of Con's unique ability to enthuse people to attend an untried project. Seán Ó Mórdha told Con that they had a success on their hands. What had been considered as a once-off event had its most recent School in August 2011. The first Winter School was held in early 1969 in Nenagh, at which Máirtín Ó Cadhain delivered his famous *Páipéir Bhána Agus Paipéir Bhreaca*. It is still an annual event and is conducted in Irish.

The first time I met Con was at the 1972 Summer School in Scariff. The theme was Daniel O'Connell and the rise of Irish Democracy. Con was on holidays from Boston and was staying at the Clare Lakelands Hotel. He was in rare form. I remember the proprietor, Seamus Treacy, double-batting an eyelid when Con requested a champagne breakfast – a new concept in east Clare. Con had booked in as 'Con Howard' but the champagne was charged to the account of 'Conchúr Ó hIomhair'. Fortunately, the management succeeded in fusing the diplopic images before the day of reckoning! Con had a most unusual personality that appealed to such disparate personalities as Rocky Marciano and Ted Heath,

Denis Donoghue and Tip O'Neill. He seemed to me to be like Michael Cusack, the extraordinary personality that emerges from Liam O'Cathnia's biography, not the Cusack of *Ulysses*.

References are often made of the enormous amounts of drinking at Merriman. There was a joke that people had drinks between lectures at Yeats and lectures between drinks at Merriman! The *Clare Champion* noted in 1974 that the School was the biggest money spinner in the history of Scariff: "A get-together for a clique who seemed determined to cling to the last vestiges of their prime and let reality slip away in an atmosphere of back-slapping camaraderie", Emer O'Kelly opined recently about even the best of the Summer Schools; "The point was to compete with each other for the floor in the course of the long evenings in the pub while downing stupefying amounts of alcohol. That, rather than the programme, was what it was all about." There is an element of truth in this. However, any reviewer of the School programme over the last 44 years in English and Irish would be astonished by the quality and diversity achieved by a small, dedicated, voluntary group, always struggling with inadequate funding. 43 scholarly works in Irish were published during this time, including the definitive version of the Merriman poem. There were other occasional publications. It is a huge cultural contribution. If people are accused of enjoying themselves in the process, so be it. There were scholarships arranged by Con in the early days of the School. The beautiful Mia Widenberg from Sweden wrote in 1972 that the School had changed her life! Nuala O'Faolain was to echo this shortly before her death when she said that Merriman had completely changed her understanding of Irish culture.

A feature of the Merriman School was the high standard of singing. John A. Murphy would not only break into song to illustrate a point in his historical seminars, but would sing for hours in the local hostelries from his superb repertoire. Many of the regular attendees had a wide range of songs in Irish and English that made for wonderful listening. Con, also, liked to perform.

His declamatory verse speaking style silenced many a rowdy pub; 'An Irish Airman Foresees His Death', 'Bingen On The Rhine' and 'Fontenoy Before The Battle' were his favourites. I always considered that he could not sing, but his rendition of 'Tommy Daly' had many admirers. Tommy Daly was a famous Clare goalkeeper, who had been a medical student with my father. He died at a young age and became the subject of a ballad by Bryan Mac Mahon. Jimmy Smyth always sang it beautifully in a semi-*sean nós* style. Con was no Jimmy Smyth, but he always claimed that he sang it for the author, who told him that it was the best rendition of his ballad that he had heard! Con's detractors would mumble that the Listowel man was either tone-deaf or just another cute Kerryman. It was written to the air of 'She Lives Beside The Anner' but Con opted for the monotone version. Certainly he sang it with fierce passion.

I was with Con in Washington on one occasion. We returned quite late to our hotel with Bob Ryan, after a reception given by Tip O'Neill for Con's entourage. Con was singing 'Tommy Daly' with gusto:

> "On the wind-swept hill of Tulla within whose breast so deep,
> With dreams of Resurrection Morn, a thousand hurlers sleep;
> And with them Tommy Daly – four yews above his head –
> On the windswept hill of Tulla, where the Claremen place their dead."

On the following morning I was checking out, and I overheard an American woman complaining that there was a Vietnamese monk chanting at three o'clock in the morning. Her husband had identified the chant as he was a Vietnam veteran. While the receptionist tried to identify the monk on her guest list, I gazed into the middle distance and looked preoccupied.

Con was director of the first two Schools, and opened the 1974 School. He was director again of the extraordinary 1976 School – a special School to mark the American Bicentennial. For ten hectic days scholarly lectures were delivered without a hitch. Many of the Merriman faithful were opposed to the idea of the School that had no connection with Thomond, but Con out-manoeuvred his opponents, myself included. A fine book, *America And Ireland, 1776 - 1976*, edited by Con and David Doyle, was published, based on the lectures delivered. One of the specially-bound books, designed by Eric Patton, would have made a handsome present for President Obama. *Go Méiriceá Siar* based on the Irish language lectures delivered, and edited by Stiofán Ó hAnnracháin, was published as a companion volume.

Con continued to attend the Merriman Schools after this, while concentrating on his new projects: Ireland and Australia; Bastille Day; The Brendan Project that hoped to stage a transatlantic boat race from Kerry to Rhode Island; the re-enactment of the Battle of Dysart O'Dea... His imagination knew no bounds. He rejoiced in the proliferation of Summer Schools based on the Merriman model. "Let a hundred flowers bloom" he would say. Unlike Mao he meant it. The worthwhile would flourish, the meretricious would fade away. The Maoist theory of perpetual revolution seemed to appeal to him. He would have liked a rapid turnover of the Merriman hierarchy, so that there would be no danger of a self-perpetuating ruling clique. He did not realise that the problem was to keep the Cumann afloat, rather than that people were clinging on to power. Con attended his last Merriman shortly before he died. He was there against medical advice, and was very ill. The imperative was to revisit past scenes of delight. He was on his own *Long Road To Ummera*. I thought of Michael Cusack's lyrical account of his last visit to Clare (*Diary Of Lughaidh Lámh Fhada*).

Con's many projects were not as disparate as they may seem: there was often a unifying theme. When he opened the Merriman Summer School in 1974, he called on the government to open up continuous dialogue with emigrants: "This could only be done through Irish institutions which could benefit from the success of Irish people abroad. These people were dedicated to Ireland and their aggressive affection should be harnessed for Ireland's maximum benefit." In the Afterword to the Bicentennial book Con wrote: "The Irish-American connection has a long and strong future. The Irish are an Atlantic people and have had from the very beginning a relationship of intimacy with the American people that is certain to continue. This does not conflict with Ireland's European responsibilities but perhaps, to some degree at least, gives the country a bridge-building role between the two continents." He would have been delighted with the Farmleigh conference when politicians finally realised the economic benefit of reaching out to the diaspora who were proud of their Irish connections. Con could claim to have played a significant role in the slow maturation of the idea.

Con was a true innovator.

## SEÁN MAC MATHÚNA
Where The Waters Fall

We were sitting on the steps of the Falls Hotel grappling with guilt about not going to the lecture, and trying to cope with the awful feeling of expectancy that romantics must endure. For all Merrimaners are hopeless romantics. They are not waiting for things to happen – for things happen – like the water falls and falls and falls. No, what they are waiting for is excitement – and that never comes, never comes, never comes. Never. It's a rule. You can convince yourself that there is a trace of excitement somewhere in a pint of stout, but after the first night at Merriman you know this is more mist off the bog.

But it is at such moments as these that Greatness makes its move. Con asked me what I was stuck in at the moment. I gave him a pack of lies about half-written plays and stories. To be a writer you must start by being a competent liar.

"No," Con said, "what are you reading at the moment?".

So I told him about Ginger's *Life Of Goldsmith* which I had brought with me to Merriman. In giving Con a quick summary of what I had read I mentioned that Goldsmith had composed his first poem at the age of six.

Con became alert immediately and wanted to know more. So I gave him the background. Goldsmith's father was a minister at the church of Kilkenny West – near Athlone – and one Sunday morning young Goldsmith sat with the congregation listening to a very boring sermon. Until they all – but not the minister – saw a rat emerge out of the ceiling and climb down the rope of the sanctuary lamp. When he got to the bottom he had to turn round and head up again, his every move followed by a grateful congregation. The minister seeing the uplifted faces was sure his sermon was having a celestial effect.

So when Goldsmith got home he composed this:

> A pious rat
> For want of stairs
> Climbed down a rope
> To say his prayers.

There was a long silence from the steps – did the water stop falling?
"I wrote a poem when I was seven!" Con said, and there was a note of defiance in his tone.
"Okay, let's have it," I said.
"I was, when a child, in Australia," Con said, "and that's where this came from:"

> Above the waves that twixt us roll
> I hear the bells of Sydney toll
> Calling me on, inviting me to
> The land of sunshine and the kangaroo.

"Did you really write that yourself?" I asked.
Con rounded on me, "Did you ask Goldsmith the same question?"
Was Con jealous? Of the poem? Goldsmith? The rat?
It was a very poetic way to end a very prosaic Merriman afternoon.

History for most people is something dead; in fact history is another word for death. But Con didn't believe in death – for him history was alive and well and bursting with potential. He wanted the whole panoply of history reborn and re-enacted. And he showed he could do it – did he not rescue Merriman from oblivion and turn him into a thriving school? And St. Brendan is on the way to recovery.

But I personally was to discover another of Con's historical projects. I met him in Bloor-Yonge in Toronto one day in the early 1980s. That's where he told me about the fact that Canadians knew nothing of their history and the proof was that even though they were invaded after the American Civil War by Fenian armies, they knew nothing about it. He brought along a Canadian academic to prove it.

"There must be some mistake, Con," the academic said, "I would have heard all about it, if it had happened."

"You didn't hear it because of the secrecy," said Con, "we Irish are the best-kept secret on the planet."

We drove down to south Ontario – not too far from Niagara, and in our efforts to find the battle sites discovered that Con was right, the Irish invasions were a best-kept secret.

We finished up in a little town called Niagara-on-the-Lake where I got lost and could find neither car nor companions. I had no way of returning to Toronto and was getting scared when suddenly I heard a miracle, somewhere someone was singing 'Tommy Daly', Con's favourite song. I traced it to a pub and there were the two – Con in fine form singing to a pub full of astonished tourists. They were positive that this was all part of the Niagara experience. But though we all loved Con, we accepted that 'Tommy Daly' was the kind of song that only a mother could love.

The academic had the jitters and was almost in tears as he begged Con to desist muttering about "a different culture over here".

But there was to be no reprieve, as Con took us through each verse to the end. And when the silence came you knew that this was the Fenian victory that Con was looking for.

There is a universe within my head which I call the Merriman universe, a place of antic orbits peopled by exotic and enriched characters, some of whom were dangerously enriched; but to the fore stands the bold Con, a character that can never be replaced. As the time goes by and as Merriman continues to be a yearly milestone we will realise that more and more, that the world is changing and that people of Con's caliber and insight are not being made anymore.

But in the Merriman universe there is very little that is certain, except that at this precise moment down there in Clare the water falls, falls and falls. If the falling waters have memories then somewhere in their gushing streams we might hear the lilt of 'Tommy Daly' delivered by an immortal Con.

# DEREK MAHON
*An Indian Garden (from Homage To Gaia)*

Indigo night fronds like
Quills dipped in ink
Share in the life cycle
As quietly as they drink

The close tropical heat.
New coconuts take shape
In clusters out of reach,
'Patrimony of the ape'

Said Durrell. A well-aimed
Machete stroke; you sip
Nectar, and the brainy
Skull is its own cup.

It rots in sandy soil
Here at the ocean rim,
Changing to coal and oil
Through geological time.

The spiritual substance
We generate likewise
Rejoins the ancient dance.
It never really dies

But circulates at random
Somewhere in the ether
When body closes down;
And so we live for ever.

From Derek Mahon's *New Collected Poems* (2011), by kind permission of the author and The Gallery Press.

## BRIAN MOONEY
The One That Got Away

In 1969, the renowned Brendan O'Regan gave my wife and myself the job of drawing up a blueprint for the indigenous-type development in the Burren in Con Howard's beloved Co. Clare. One of the windfalls that came our way at the time – a story in itself – was what is known as Tullycommon, the best Winterage in the Burren.

Winterages are winter grasslands unique to the Burren. You can put cattle in there in November and you don't have to worry about them until the following May. Tullycommon was more than just a good winterage. It also contained one of the best tracts – some would claim the best tract – of hazel woodland in Europe. This made one particular section of it relatively useless for farm purposes. But, in the Burren, hazel acts as cover for wild animals like the fox, badger, pine marten and stoat. As most of these animals are nocturnal, they are not that visible during the day. But the idea slowly grew of a Radio-Telemetric Centre. The animals would be tagged or bugged with electronic signals. These signals would feed into a central building where they would show up as blips on a screen. Certain sections of the hazel would also be covered by infra-red cameras fortifying the blips with live pictures.

It was at this stage I met Con. The idea fired his imagination straight away... He was in like a shot. Kevin Lynch, the world-renowned Boston architect of Irish descent would design 'The Dome' into which the pictures and blips would be fed. It would be a building to command world interest and respect. As for money, that would be no problem. Con would organise a meeting in the Irish Embassy in London which would bring the right people together to finance it. He would contact Kevin Lynch for preliminary sketches. These would be presented at the meeting in London. The right people would be invited. And they were.

It was a time when sensitivities to environment were not paramount. However, I remember at that meeting Sidney Nolan's wife, Mary, had a problem with the possible environmental impact of The Dome, in such a fragile setting. The excitement of the project had carried us all away a little and so we did not pay that much attention to her. Her fears were to prove well grounded. We had, in fact, unknowingly, stumbled on a Mullaghmore-type project, which meant, ultimately, the whole idea had to be scrapped. So, this was one of Con Howard's projects that got away. But how well it sums up the spirit of the man: alive to and fired by the imaginative idea, aware of what needed to be done to make it work, knowing the people who needed to be contacted and bringing the whole thing about with his own particular panache.

How to really describe him? Human? Passionate? Imaginative? Fulsome? True? None of these words seem to do him justice. There is one word that comes to mind. It is – glorious.

## MIKE MOONEY
Carousing On Capitol Hill

In the 1980s and 1990s, ambassadors came and went, some going up the ladder and some going down, but Con Howard seemed to go on forever.

He held court every Friday afternoon at the Irish Times or at the Dubliner, bars which were run by Hughie Kelley and Danny Coleman, respectably and respectively.

It wasn't easy to get a prolonged hearing with Con unless you were prepared to spend the whole afternoon and some part of the evening too, awaiting your audience. We had come miles from the suburbs to talk to Con, to listen to him recite, to sing with him and to get our orders for the coming week. I wish Yeats had never written, 'An Irish Airman Foresees His Death'. Con couldn't be dissuaded.

Con was a great supporter of everything Irish and Gaelic, especially the GAA. He was at school at St. Flannan's in Ennis. His school was the pre-eminent college hurling team in Munster and he never ceased rubbing it in to unfortunates like the Christian Brothers boys from Thurles who hadn't won the Harty Cup in 56 years.

Once, while we were reminiscing about our days at UCD, we regretted we didn't have something like the Literary and Historical Society over here like we attended religiously every Saturday night in the early 1950s. Con decided to do something about it.

Even though we were thousands of miles away we determined to start our own society here on Capitol Hill in DC. I wanted to call it the 'Red Branch Knights' with membership limited to people who could remove a thorn from the foot while in flight over a fence like the knights of old.

Con shot that down and decided we should call ourselves the 'Capitol Hill Cultural and Carousing Society', catering to the diaspora in America.

For premises to meet in, Con arranged through his friend Congressman James Howard that we could use the Gold Room in the Rayburn Building: a beautifully appointed room that could seat 75 listeners at tables where each table had a microphone which we could switch on and off if we needed to interrupt the speaker like the old days at Earlsfort Terrace in Dubin. We were merciless with any poor speaker who left big gaps in his delivery, shouting from the gods, "In the interval we will play you a gramophone record".

Our opening night was to feature Senator Eugene McCarthy, Democrat from Minnesota, lecturing on WB Yeats. McCarthy was accompanied by a bevy of pretty college girls. Yeats' poetry went out the window and he substituted his own poems for the master's. Still, it was a great success and a wonderful party ensued at the *Dubliner*. Con was ecstatic. Another great triumph. He was ready for Broadway.

Great success followed for several years, with famous personalities vying for an opportunity to address the Capitol Hill Cultural and Carousing Society. But the inevitable end was near. Con was going home, his long vexations past, there to await his pension at last.

The question of Con's successor was to be settled at a meeting at Hughie Kelly's town house. At the last moment before the voting started, a Jewish girl, Ann Rabinotitz, stated that she objected to my candidacy saying, "There are things in Mike's background which if they came to light would reflect adversely on the Carousing Society. Not wishing to cause a rift in the society, I withdrew from the race asking but one question of Bernie Clancy who worked for the

Teamsters Union.

"Bernie, is there anything in your background that would bring disrepute on the Capitol Hill Cultural and Carousing Society?"

Quick as a flash he replied, "They never found Jimmy Hoffa did they?"

# BRENDAN Ó CATHAOIR
A Clareman Through And Through

Love of the Burren region defined our friendship. My last encounter with Con involved presenting him with a copy of *Clare: History And Society*. He spoke with acuity about my contribution: a chapter of social and family history.

It occasioned a celebratory lunch in Bray. Con remembered my uncle, Francis Cahir, who lost the sight of an eye when he and my father were ambushed on their winterage in Carron in 1925 (coincidentally, the year of Con's birth). He knew one of the three men charged with (but not convicted of) the shooting. Jack Irwin was capable of both kindness and savagery, Con recalled, in what would have been a commonplace remark in any other context. I regretted not having talked to him before writing about the incident.

For Con was a raconteur worth recording. He spoke of his days in the Boston consulate, of his friendship with President Kennedy – they remained friends until JFK's assassination – and with former world heavyweight boxing champion Rocky Marciano.

The sage of the Burren, John O'Donohue (1956 – 2008), said: "Friendship is the grace which warms and sweetens our lives ... Friendship is the nature of God."

Con was an amiable, astute, ebullient Clareman. Although unpretentious, he possessed limitless self-belief. He felt nothing was beyond his powers. By force of personality he opened the doors of the White House to official Ireland. Furthermore, he was the father of Cumann Merriman, the initiator of the British-Irish Association, and the power behind the Society of St. Brendan.

Cumann Merriman stalwart Diarmuid Breathnach observed: "Bhí

an-mhisneach aige." In 1976 Con organised a Merriman summer school to celebrate the American Declaration of Independence, which included contributions from leading scholars working on Irish America.

He shared Barack Obama's philosophy: "Is féidir linn." The greatest representative of the Banner County, Daniel O'Connell, loved to quote Byron: "Hereditary bondsmen, know ye not, who would be free themselves must strike the blow?"

Like another north Clare person – the magnificent Mary (Neylon) Hanley (1914 –79), Con was generous in encouraging others. Coole was destroyed out of ignorance and lack of imagination. Thoor Ballylee, the home of WB Yeats and overlooking the Burren, was saved by the energy and pertinacity of Mary Hanley, president of the Kiltartan Society.

Con's circle of friends included Sir Sidney Nolan, whose father's people came from Clare. In 1986 the Australian artist presented seven of his paintings to the Irish people.

Con and I sailed to Boston once for a seminar on the American Civil War. My most vivid memory is of New England in the fall, which Kennedy described as the most beautiful place in the world.

Our forum was the University of Massachusetts at Amherst, a town associated with the poet Emily Dickinson, who wrote:

> "Because I could not stop for death
> He kindly stopped for me;
> The carriage held but just ourselves
> And immortality."

Fr. Tom Stack, who celebrated Con's funeral mass, recalled the enthusiasm and sense of adventure of a loyal friend. He described him as an engaging storyteller, who was socially inventive: "Con could start things which he sometimes didn't finish." Unfinished business included a re-enactment of the voyage of the *Catalpa*, the whaling ship used to rescue six Fenian prisoners from a penal settlement in Western Australia on Easter Monday, 1876.

Con's favourite song, 'The Lament For Tommy Daly', was sung by Clare hurling legend, Jimmy Smyth.

The Burren has been a habitat for herdsmen and an inspiration to mystics. Colman Mac Duach, the seventh century saint, was the first to render this place "susceptible to the presence of heaven".

Mention of heaven recalls jazz composer Mary Lou Williams, who declared: "Heaven isn't our reward, but our rest. And the rest is better when you've earned it." Con earned his rest.

## ULICK O'CONNOR
A Celtic Prince Out For A Walk

Con was one of the outstanding figures in Dublin from the 1960s onwards. His colossal energy and ability for organisation made him a formidable figure in the Department of Foreign Affairs. Outside his diplomatic duties he was responsible for the creation of two outstanding organisations, the Merriman School and the Brendan Society. His energy, vitality and knowledge all combined to make both bodies remarkable organisations, where people of different backgrounds could get together and explore aspects of Irish culture and heritage. His other love was the Arts Club. There was nothing he couldn't do for it. I do think there were periods in the last decades of the twentieth century when the club might well have foundered had it not been for Con's energy and ability to hold people together. He had enormous generosity and was always prepared to forgive people who had harmed him and continue on a new basis of friendship. Like all great people he had the elements of an eccentric. To see him walking into town on a Sunday afternoon all the way from Mount Merrion with a giant Afghan dog reminded one of a Celtic prince out for a walk among his subjects.

One of Con's striking characteristics was that he didn't nourish grudges. From time to time, because of his energy and exuberance, certain people envied him and set about trying to undermine many of the projects he had initiated. He refused, however, to indulge in the luxury of begrudgery. He was more concerned with getting on with whatever project he was involved in than seeking revenge on those who would try to undo him.

Not the least of his characteristics was enormous courage. He refused to be subdued by infirmity and carried on for years as if it didn't exist. It is fair to say that if Con hadn't remained in the Arts Club – injecting his gift for organisation and management of projects – it would be a lesser place today.

We will think of him in the years to come whenever qualities of loyalty, generosity and tenacity are required to achieve a goal.

## AIDAN O'HARA
He Made The Best Of This

Con had a small boy's delight in seeing others enjoying themselves. Although he was the one who got them all together in the first place, very often no-one was having more fun than himself. But behind the gaiety and *bonhomie* was a man of wide learning and experience who was ever alert and on the ball. He was an amazing combination of talker and action man, ever ready to take up even a casual observation on the part of one of the company, throw the idea around and see what emerged.

It was like that when he asked me to meet him at his 'local' in Stillorgan, Co. Dublin, some time in the late 1980s. His idea was to do something on the Irish in the era of the American Civil War, and he felt that a book on the subject with contributions from leading Irish and American historians was what was needed.

About the year 1990, I was at a function in Dublin organised by Con, and afterwards I wrote to a friend telling him all about it. "It's certainly only a Con Howard who could bring together a gathering like this that includes pen-pushers, and poets, politicians and professors. If his friend, Fr. Tom Stack had been there, of course, I'd be able to maintain the alliterative listing and include the priests."

Con had a great fondness for poetry and verse and would have loved these lines of Robert Burns, written about a dear departed friend. The words of the Bard of Ayrshire express my sentiments for Con:

> "Few hearts like his, with virtue warm'd,
> Few heads with knowledge so informed;
> If there is another world, he lives in bliss;
> If there is none, he made the best of this."

## SEÁN Ó MÓRDHA
An Ideal Man

An t-Éireannach Ildánach – the multi-talented Irishman – is a much abused cliché. By common consent, and with appreciation, Con Howard passes the test. Blessed with good health, gifted with physical and intellectual energy, he was in every sense a force of nature. Con Howard could lay claim to have been the most unorthodox public servant in the Irish diplomatic service. The way he went about his duties was, shall we say, different. He managed to work within the system while at all times being his individual self. With immense creativity he bent the rules without breaking the rules.

Fundamentally, Con was an ideas man. Some ideas were quite splendid, others quite daft, all were pursued with the Howard brand of relentless energy and enthusiasm. A great walker, he often took 20-mile tracks in the hills at weekends, contemplating projects and ideas that would come to haunt us all when the Howard momentum moved into top gear.

Con Howard's native Clare, its people and its culture was the motivating force of his life. He was the founder and the great driving force behind Cumann Merriman, a public expression of his private self. Who will forget his war cry of encouragement, Con's Clare shout –

> "Let the forwards do their duty
> and the backs we'll back them up
> and back to Ennis we'll bring
> The Doctor Harty Cup."

Looking back over his many achievements the one that always stands out for me was his supervision of the Irish American Bicentennial celebration in 1976 and the superb book published to commemorate that historic event. This was Con at his most magnificent. The contributions to *America And Ireland 1776 – 1976* by Denis Donoghue, John A. Murphy, Lawrence McCaffrey, Thomas N. Brown and Michael Ó hAodha are in their own way personal tributes to their great friend Con Howard.

# ROSEMARIE ROWLEY
*For Con Howard*

A skipper for the Irish ship of state
He launched us into adventure so fast
When the future was derailed, up for debate
He nailed our colours proudly to the mast –

We tacked with Brendan as the first mate
On the clear Atlantic sprawl our net was cast
Through sparkling seas that redefined our fate
To bring to light those treasures that last;

Cultural, linguistic: Con to navigate
Our rule or role, and refreshing repast,
Our minds, once nightmare of hate,
Enriched now, sailed to morning, not overcast

But bright and bold to make a future state
Of knowledge; and we were rescued from our past.

## DESMOND RUSHE
A Born Communicator

There are two instances which spring to mind when reflecting on Con Howard's extraordinary talent as a communicator: the ease with which he could establish meaningful and lasting relationships on every conceivable level was astonishing.

In the first instance, there was the case of Edward Richard George Heath. Remarkably, he and Con became close friends. A profound rapport developed between them. They clearly liked and trusted each other, and were on first-name terms – Ted and Con. The circumstances surrounding the formation and development of the relationship made it special.

Ted became leader of the Conservative party in the late 1960s, and Prime Minister in 1970, an office he held for four years. It was a period of depressing violence and bloodshed in the North of Ireland – including Bloody Sunday – and it was also a time of intense Anglo-Irish diplomatic activity. Con was attached to the Irish embassy in London and was busy using the legendary Howard charm in political and media circles. I was very surprised when he told me, some years later, that the person he remembered with most affection and esteem from the period was Ted Heath.

From his first meeting with him at a social function, Con said, Ted Heath showed a sincere, sympathetic and open-minded desire to come to grips with the many, subtle and ancient intricacies inherent in the Irish question. And although Con did not say so, perhaps it was because of his influence that the Prime Minister sent a SIS officer to hold secret meetings with the Provisional IRA in 1971 and instructed Northern Secretary Willie Whitelaw to hold unofficial talks with the PIRA in London a year later.

The Heath premiership saw the suspension of the Stormont parliament, the imposition of direct British rule in the North and a general worsening of Anglo-Irish relations. Yet, it also saw the first Sunningdale Agreement with its breakthrough power-sharing agenda: it was sabotaged by Unionist intransigence but, years later, its provisions formed the basis for much of the Good Friday Agreement. Con's friend could take some of the credit for that. Heath was succeeded as Prime Minister in 1974 by the devious, pipe-smoking Harold Wilson, and as Tory leader by the execrable Thatcher woman in 1975.

Wilson and Thatcher did not rank among the people Con chose to remember with fondness: with Ted Heath it was different, and when Con founded the Brendan Society – Tim Severin having proved that the Navigator could have discovered America, and probably did – he invited friend Ted to become its Vice President. The invitation was accepted with pleasure.

The second instance which springs to mind has a different geographical location. On March 30, 1981, an assassination attempt on President Ronald Reagan was made outside the Hilton Hotel in Washington. While the attempt failed, there was a non-fatal casualty when the White House Press Secretary, Jim Brady, suffered a serious head wound. He was partially paralysed and his speech, when he could speak at all, was slurred. For a time it was doubted if he would survive. I happened to be in Washington at the time, and I saw Con Howard's devastation first hand. He was Jim Brady's closest friend and, because of that friendship, he was well known to the President.

Quite by accident and because of my contact with Con, I was at a St. Patrick's Day lunch in the Irish embassy in Washington a few years later. President Reagan was there and I spoke to him about his upcoming visit to Ireland. He mentioned how musical his ancestral village of Ballyporeen sounded, and when I made a passing reference to Jim Brady, he said that Con Howard had proved himself an extremely good friend to the Press Secretary and his family.

Perhaps he had heard that a Mass for Jim Brady's well-being had been celebrated in the chapel of Dublin Castle: it was arranged by Con and among the invited congregation was Brian Lenihan, the elder, who was Minister for Foreign Affairs at the time. He, of course, had known Con well, and he added his name to the list of well-wishers which went from the Castle chapel to the Brady family. The Mass was typical of Howard's thoughtfulness and concern in regard to his countless legions of friends.

# ROSE RUSHE
Viva, Me-hico

After the overnight helicopter swoops and shoot-outs between cops and robbers in Mexico City, we knew Oaxaca was going to be a different scene, sunnier, freer, with expectations of exotica and desert scents swaying our thoughts. Our thinking was also swayed by the sudden fatal shooting of a police officer as our coach pulled into town.

Our seven serene days staying in Oaxaca's Mision de los Angelos, a converted convent with tropical grounds, was a time of Irish art, publication, gun salutes and celebratory food together around the Zocola Square. We danced to mariachi bands under orange blossom. We combed the acres of markets, wandered the town for silver and coral, sucked cactus liquor from pods and worshipped evening finery at the weddings of Mexico's elite in the golden church of Santa Domingo.

There are layers to latter-day Mexico as much as to its archaeological past, some vicious. Fear crackled in the town, like that rifle shot from a drugs cartel, followed by a new regard on our part for the mantle of St. Brendan.

Such was the nature of our travels as the saint's self-elected voyagers of the 20th century. Annual explorations of the wonders created by Irish holy men and scholars and journeymen took place overseas, from Iona to America to Australia. Ploughing in the wake of founding members Con Howard and Mary Caulfield to spend St. Patrick's Days in countries remarkable for their connection with the ancient and everyday Irish, we always managed a safe passage within the troubled histories shared.

Con was the visionary, Mary our wordsmith and deft organiser.

Someone else drove the bus, but the agenda was Con's in his steadfast recovery and gathering of Irish heritage and present culture abroad. For younger people on board like me, so much of this was discovery for the first time, his lantern to the window of the world.

We travelled first to Mexico City in September, 2002 to celebrate St. Patrick's Day by way of the September 12 annual celebration of the San Patricio Batallan. This battalion was led in the 1840s by a bold Connemara man, John Reilly.

Our day in Mexico was long planned. Con had been a huge favourite of Ambassador Agnew and his most able and friendly first secretary Sheila Maguire. They received our party at the Embassy immediately to wise us on security. A list of directives followed: Never take a cab on the street or even from outside our Krystal Rosa Hotel haven. Never. Stay with your guide. Do not walk around alone. Know that Mexico is a city in which metro transport is segregated by gender to help safeguard the women. Summon the wrong cab and find yourself locked in the boot at gunpoint, your money stolen and your lifespan as short as how long it takes to empty your credit card at the ATM.

Embassy staff supplied us with their list of safe numbers, and extracted vows of obedience as to solidarity and safekeeping. Fortified, we barreled along on our itinerary to see Trotsky's home, a living museum. We climbed the Pyramid of the Sun and the Pyramid of the Moon, and ventured deep in buried civilisations at Teotihuacan and its sacrificial chambers.

On we went to track the story of Mexico's evolution through epic murals of Diego Rivera and Frida Kahlo around the city's zocola, folk tales writ large in coloured fury for Mexican peoples who could not read. On then to Kahlo's pretty house and her bucking against the strait-jackets of illness and convention.

Our guide secured for Mexico by Con was the wise and honest Sergio, an esoteric who loved his country magnificently despite its sores. He was rumoured to be 80, looked a wiry, alert 60, and was worried about the arrival of his latest baby. We were awestruck.

Sergio just about coped with the pilgrimage to Our Lady of Guadalupe, roses entwined between her black feet. He brought the pyramids to life, and their layers of Mayan and Aztec cultures, and kept the hawkers tethered. He told us why the Dominican order was known as the Dogs of God for setting on the indigenous races so savagely. A week into his Irish travels, Sergio had versed us in esotericism, his tool for making sense of Mexico's chopped-up, bricked-up history, the avid gore of drug wars and cruelty at the US border.

Further Irish-Mexican links were celebrated at the yearly military commemoration of the San Patricios. We joined full-colour troops on the commemorative September 12 for the national salute to John Reilly (Seán O'Raghailligh in his native Clifden) who turned around to train his gun on the Americans while engaged to fight against Mexico for the US army.

The Mexican-American War (1846-1848) saw America expanding downwards by taking Arizona, California, and New Mexico from Mexico. Mexico was at that stage a vast territorial swathe from coast to coast, its imperial splendour extended back to Aztec times of successive, sophisticated civilisations.

The later conquistadors had come with their racks of torture, bayonets and the decimating foul of sexual diseases. Having come through that, Mexico could not wish to cede against an America stir-crazy with its fear of black slave liberation.

The 19th century carnage was shocking in this rape of Mexico by North America. Reilly, and his circa 175 immigrant Catholic men and slaves, downed arms in battle, refusing to kill Mexicans struggling to retain land and title against the oppressor. Changing allegiance, they became national heroes for Mexico and strove against US oppression. The parallel with our own colonial history was too much for them to bear arms against the underdog.

Captain Reilly, who left an account of the battalion, noted the St. Patrick's Battalion flag:

> "In all my letter, I forgot to tell you under what banner we fought so bravely. It was that glorious emblem of native rights, that being the banner which should have floated over our native soil many years ago, it was St. Patrick, the Harp of Erin, the Shamrock upon a green field."

The members of Reilly's battalion that survived the war were ultimately sentenced, without defence, for treason, and most were hung. Hanging was at that time considered a death fit only for "spies without uniform and atrocities against civilians", but these were not charges brought against them. One man, Francis O'Connor, was hung although he had had his legs amputated the previous day. Such was the American lust for exemplary vengeance.

Today, the Connemara town of Clifden flies the Mexican flag on September 12 in honour of its son, Reilly. The St. Patrick's Battalion 1847 plaque has pride of place in Mexico, engraved with the names of Martin Lydon, John Bartely, David McElroy, Patrick Casey and dozens more.

That September 12 in 2002 was, I'd swear, among Con Howard's finest as founder of St. Brendan Society of voyagers. Flanked by Mary, he was front row guest, in with ambassadors and governors and clergy, as Mexican troops marched with Irish, San Patricio and Mexican flags in full gun salute. Ireland's hero in Mexico was made vibrant and real to us through Con's offices.

It would be wrong, deeply wrong, to recall our eight days in the 18 million capital stronghold and not light a halo over clothes designer Jimmy Hourihan. A good sort, if ever, he travelled with us and kept us whole. Any night not spent in the company of army or ambassadorial grandees, Jimmy beckoned after his notes on restaurant life, notes culled from a previous time there selling Hourihan luxuriates to South American airports. By night we would sally to his call and be secured a fabulous table with his okay Spanish and fabulous charm. *Comer en la terraza* – dining on Mexican terraces – was powerful stuff then. We sang, well, Mary Caulfield and Con and Harry Farrell did, told our stories in Irish and English, and toasted la viva Me-hi-co.

Pueblo? God forgive me, I can only recall a verdant oval in the city centre that was as long as the rain that fell. In shoulder-softening contrast to Mexico city's intensity, Oaxaca was a carnival week after that. Much that was good and Irish was happening. Like me, I think Con slept a lot and powered up for the next station, our week in Oaxaca.

Picture St. Brendan's busload arriving, and Eoin Mac Donagh pushing Con's wheelchair through hot sandy streets, or nursing Con's halt of a walk. Although they followed us, Con Howard always led, usually singing ballads off-key.

Louis Le Broquy's pen and ink drawings that illustrated *An Táin* were brought in from Ireland to create a visual show parallel with the launch of the first translation of *An Táin* into Spanish. The story of bulls locking territories, its allegory and strength, is loved by Hispanics. We were in Oaxaco in force to relish this international homage to our classics, and gawp at Anne Madden's stand-alone exhibition of fiery, beautiful oils on monstrous canvas. The artwork was stunning, displayed in the old Spanish-style mansions, their cool courtyards a welcome retreat off the dusty camino.

Reader, you will have guessed that not all our moments in Mexico were so historic in the high-minded sense. There were happy nights dancing in Mision de los Angelos nightclub with waiters on table tops, ridiculously handsome men who used their aprons as bull capes to fire the temp. Viva Me-hi-co some more? Oh, yes, and viva Enrique Iglesias, Gloria Estefan and her Miami Sound Machine Band, viva mariachi sombreros and our own *mision* as St. Brendan's angels with dirty faces, having the time of our lives.

There was hot chocolate *mole* for breakfasts, afternoons on margaritas by the pool, shawls of gold and greens in the markets, jewellery and jade bangles to weigh down the wrists. Con loved the colourful parade of life in this southern town: gypsies passing by, stack-heeled drug merchants, American camera tourists, *policias* with gunbelts, European stragglers with dilated eyes, flower sellers bearing jasmine. We sat around nursing espresso on the terraces of this theatre of life.

At 8pm of an evening, the wedding belles would shimmer out from Santa Domingo's splendour in finery, threads of gold and silver against the silver apples of moon, the golden apples of the sun. We were there to romance their romance and strategic alliances and then, one day we looked up at the sky beyond the spires and found that the moon was Silvermine silver. St. Brendan, Con and Mary had spirited us back over the ocean.

Mexico was one in a series of relentless voyagers' adventures from the United Arts Club in Merrion Square. Everyone was meshed through Con's former roles in Foreign Affairs but God knows, he never lorded it.

Exploring the sacred sights, caves and temples of Sri Lanka was another telling lesson in past meets present. With 'Journalist' stamped on my passport I was taken aside on entry point to Colombo and quizzed aggressively by Uzi-bearing security. Mary worked faithfully for my 'extradition' from the armed ones with her documentation explaining the honorary mission of St. Brendan Society of voyagers. Our patron saint, Brendan interceded as much as Mary's professionalism. Because of state media censorship, we had to wait until we returned to Ireland to read off the Press Association wire that hundreds had been killed in the Tamil Tiger versus state army bush-fighting during our fortnight crossing the country. Our connection with Sri Lanka had been Con's former post as Irish honorary consul, but due to ill health, he had to pull out of that trip.

Reader, this book is full of adventures around the globe and politics in the spirit of sharing, arriving at knowledge, and realising the diversity and courage of the Irish diaspora over centuries and even today. Thank God and Con and Mary Caulfield for that.

Now turn another page. The dance goes on.

\* *Viva, Me-hico* is the motto inscribed on the mantle of the St. Brendan Society.

## BOB RYAN
An extract from *With A Tap On The Knee*

Some of the friends I made through my job were truly extraordinary people, one or two of them defying all the laws of convention. One day in Merrion Row, I ran into Con Howard, whom I had first met in London when he was attached to the Irish embassy as counsellor in charge of media relations, a post created by the government in 1970 to help counteract the negative publicity being generated by the violence in Northern Ireland and the arms trial in Dublin.

Con was a legendary figure not only in Dublin and London, but also in Washington and in Boston, where he had begun his diplomatic career as consul general. I had barely set foot in London before I began to be asked, 'Have you met Con Howard yet?' On replying in the negative, I was invariably advised to make it my business to do so without delay.

I phoned the embassy, made an appointment and went along, not quite knowing what to expect. It turned out to be like encountering someone who had just experienced a beatific vision. Barely introduced, I was swept off to The King And Keys, where I was immediately swallowed up in his enthusiasm for his latest project, the St. Brendan Society. Before I had time to draw breath, I found that I had become a member of the steering committee. It was hard to be sure what I was getting into, but I did discover that this distinguished body had been inspired by Con's friendship with Tim Severin, who had recreated St. Brendan's epic voyage to Newfoundland and had subsequently written the bestseller, *The Brendan Voyage*. Con was determined that the spirit of St. Brendan would be kept alive, and he outlined a dizzying array of ideas he had conceived for events and activities to be organized with the goal of furthering Irish-American social and cultural ties.

In the pub, I was introduced by Con to the essayist and powerful political editor of the *Daily Telegraph*, Peter TE Utley, a Tory whose virulent anti-Irish views did nothing to protect him from being co-opted immediately to the St. Brendan Society's steering committee. We were also joined by the *Telegraph*'s gardening expert, Douglas Watson, a former Jesuit who wore a red rose in his buttonhole and began chanting Latin psalms at the sight of Con. 'Ah, Watson! You'll be coming too – you're on the committee!' declared Con, before breaking into his trademark anthem, the many-versed 'Ballad Of Tommy Daly' by Bryan MacMahon, delivered by Con in the sort of powerful tremolo voice that shatters windows in Marx Brothers films.

> *And from the broken northlands*
> *From the Burren bleak and bare*
> *The dirge of Tommy Daly*
> *Goes surging on through Clare.*

(I once heard Tip O'Neill, former US Speaker of Congress, describe Con's rendering of this ballad as doubtful singing, but definitely an art form.)

In my next recollection of that evening, it is after midnight and we have all adjourned to the upper floors of the *Telegraph*'s offices where we have joined the paper's night workers in their canteen. Heaped plates of sausages and mash are being washed down by copious quantities of brown ale. Interestingly, the knives and forks are attached to the tables by chains. Con – who boasts an ample frontage which, like its owner, always seems to be about to burst free of restraint – is now standing on a table, from where, having won the hearts of his cockney audience with the exploits of Tommy Daly, he is busy recruiting new members to the St. Brendan Society. He assures them that it has the support of the former British Prime Minister, Edward Heath, who has, it seems, been persuaded to chair one of its supporting committees (sailing section). By now, I am ready to believe him... and sure enough, some years later a member of the staff of the *Irish Times* who had met Ted Heath confirmed to me that the Tory politician had actually raised the matter with him.

If I digress with this story, it is because it contains some of the elements of the surreal which I soon discovered to be a defining characteristic of Con's many inventions, among them the Merriman and Shaw Summer Schools, the Byron Society and the Ireland-Australian Society. All his causes are promoted with the same terrifying missionary zeal. It is impossible to put a boundary around the imagination of Con Howard, scourge of bureaucrats and the mandarins of decorum in the Department of Foreign Affairs. It is also easy to underestimate the value of what he has achieved for Ireland through the wheels he has set in motion and friendships forged. It was largely due to Con that Ireland received an important bequest of paintings from the great Australian artist, Sir Sidney Nolan. In all the years I have known him, I have never heard him bad-mouth anyone, and it is suspected that much of the finance for his ventures came from his own pocket.

But to return to our encounter in Merrion Row, both our London interludes now well behind us. As soon as Con spotted me, he prepared to hijack me with his latest project. This involved building a replica of the *Catalpa*, the four-masted whaling ship involved in the rescue of Fenians from the penal colony in Australia. My assistance was apparently needed. Con outlined the plot in his usual breathless shorthand.

'Epic voyage – re-enactment – financial backing – Tuesday, three o'clock – the *Asgard* – Alexandra Basin. Be there!'

I gazed at his cherubic countenance: the ruddy cheeks, disheveled white hair, demented bushy eyebrows shooting skywards in oblique lines. Con was always deadly serious about his schemes, even if his earnestness was regularly punctuated by manic bursts of laughter.

'Sounds terrific, Con,' I said (although some of the details had in fact passed me by).

'So you're with us then?'

'Well…'

'Good man, good man.' He added: 'O'Reilly's coming! – he's putting up millions!' (Con also had a dream about making a film based on the *Catalpa* adventure, and he was attempting to persuade various potential backers – among them Tony O'Reilly – to put up the money. Unfortunately, Con's enthusiasm would sometimes lead him to confuse the reality of what had been agreed with the desired outcome.)

The tide was out the following Tuesday as I walked down the quayside towards the *Asgard* and stared at what looked like an empty ship. Boarding, I heard a murmur of voices coming from the captain's quarters.

'You're late,' Con grumbled, as he introduced me to a dozen men of distinction from the marine world, who seemed pleased to meet me and shook my hand vigorously. Strewn across the table were architectural drawings of a sailing ship. The chief concern was whether the hull should be of steel or wood. After some debate, steel was decided upon, at a cost of some £7m. The eyes of the distinguished gathering turned to me.

'What do you think?' someone asked. I told him I thought it was a wonderful idea.

'Well, not so much that,' he said, 'but the money. Will the financial support be forthcoming, do you think? Will it be okay?'

The question took me by surprise. 'It's a bit outside by area,' I replied, 'but it's certainly worth making an approach to the bank.'

There was a brief silence.

'But,' someone finally asked, 'aren't you the chief executive?'

'Who, me?' I turned to Con, who seemed busy with a flurry of papers. 'O'Reilly,' he muttered. 'O'Reilly's the man'.

For all I know, the *Catalpa II* may be on the high seas even as I write.

# TOM STACK
A Romantic Par Excellence

With Con Howard there was always something happening. Up to the end, he was ever full of unusual projects; often of a commemorative kind, either of special persons or of singular bygone events. These were always driven by a celebratory motif. In this respect his enthusiasm was perennial.

With Con one might travel on picaresque journeys. I had the good fortune of sharing the odd one of these experiences. I remember in particular one such outing in the autumn of 1973; I found myself in New York for a meeting to do with Catholic Communications which, at the last minute, was postponed for three days. During this period of unexpected free time I decided to visit Con who was then Irish Consul General in Boston. This plan he duly welcomed with his usual gusto, adding that he was, just then, as it happened, on vacation at a holiday cottage in the Berkshire Mountains in Massachusetts. He instructed me to travel up by Pilgrim Airways (bargain price!) to be met by him at Bradley Field near Hartford, Connecticut; from where we would journey to the Berkshires. Complying, I joined Con at our rendezvous where I then heard the real story of his immediate schedule, which involved traipsing, it seemed, around most of New England during the rest of the evening. As ever, Con's elaborate timetable was surprising and I suspected then that his proposed itinerary was indeed logistically impossible. However..!

Con then told me that he had been due to give an address on 'Irish Culture' to a large gathering of young Americans from Worcester University, who had convened at the residence of their professor, one Rhona Fields. This venue was some 30 miles away and we were already running late. On our eventual arrival at Dr. Fields' home we encountered some 30 'Irish Studies' students, who by then, had been plied by their academic hostess with large draughts of Jameson whiskey while awaiting the Consul General's anticipated lecture. Con excused his late arrival by announcing that he had been delayed in order to collect a visitor who had flown from New York, an Irish priest who was 'an expert on Church and State in Ireland'! That was Con's compensatory flourish. The stirring session concluded with a short contribution from yours truly. Con then confided to me that he had promised to take Rhona Fields out to dinner after the 'scholastic session' had ended. The three of us set out for a favourite roadhouse restaurant called Timothy Twos, quite a distance away. When finally we reached this establishment, the staff had stacked the chairs away, and were about to close for the night, but Con's arrival miraculously transformed the scene. The proprietor and waiters joined in a splendid repast, now for some reason being referred to as 'a celebratory dinner'. Sometime later, after toasts to Irish/American friendship we were of course obliged to transport Professor Fields back to her home. Next, Con announced that he had to drive all the way back to Boston to leave a cheque, due to the cleaning lady at the premises of the Consulate there. (Con being officially on vacation in the Berkshires would not be in the office the next day)

On our high speed drive to Boston we came upon a car crash on the freeway. Having established that the driver and passengers were relatively unscathed, we resumed our journey. By now we were in the small hours of the morning. We made it to Boston however, and, eventually, having left the cheque as planned, we set out for Con's holiday cottage in the Berkshires.

Beginning to feel drowsy on route, Con suggested pulling in to a lay-by deep in the mountains, there to have a short snooze. Shortly I was awakened by a torch shone on me through the car window by a uniformed gentleman in a wide-brimmed hat, who turned out to be a member of an Interstate police patrol. We were suspects! But following a parley with our stern interrogators, Con's consular immunity allowed us to proceed in freedom.

It was getting bright when we reached our destination; a neat mountain chalet overlooking a lake and close to a jetty at which a rowing boat was berthed. Indefatigable as ever, Con proposed a short trip on the lake before retiring. So we rowed away while breaking into an echoing rendition of that stirring martial air well know to Clare men; *Rosc Catha Na Mumhan*. I can still recall the rhythm between our oarsmanship and the song.

After a mini circle of the lake we climbed back out of our boat, slipped quietly into the cottage and slept the 'sleep of the just'. Next day further adventures ensued, *ach sin scéal eile…!*

Con Howard was a romantic par excellence. His instinct was quixotic and his friendships were forever honoured from a heart that was both constant and generous. It was good and fitting that he once again breathed his own Clare air, shortly before he left us '*ar shlí na fírinne*'.

## MARY STOKES
Con And The Society of St. Brendan

It was mid-summer when Con organised a trip to Scotland. I can't remember the year – was it the late 1980s or the early 1990s? In keeping with his interest in establishing links between the ancient and the modern, Con had established the Society of St. Brendan in honour of St. Brendan of Clonfert (c. 484 – c. 577) or Brendan the Navigator as he is known.

Brendan was a famous voyager. The literature tells us of his legendary journey over seven years to the Isle of the Blessed, or Paradise. On his journey he encounters the wonders and the horrors of the world. Many believe that St. Brendan was the first European to reach America, and Tim Severin had shown that this was possible when he crossed the Atlantic in a replica boat. One of Brendan's journeys took him to Iona.

Lying one mile from the coast of Mull in the Inner Hebrides off the west coast of Scotland, Iona was then part of the Irish kingdom of Dál Riada. Here, his contemporary St. Columba, or Colm Cille, had journeyed from Lough Foyle with 12 clansmen to establish a monastery, about the year 563. Colm Cille is an important personage, a member of the O'Neills of Ulster, one of Ireland's ruling dynasties. He is a man of influence, who can appeal to the king of Dál Riada for assistance in his mission.

The monastery grew to become a renowned centre for learning, and its scriptorium produced many important documents. Some say that the Book of Kells may have been produced, at least in part, there.

Following in these footsteps Con and his fellow voyagers travelled by way of ferry from Larne in Northern Ireland to Stranraer in Scotland, and then on to the University of Stirling. There, a conference on Scottish Gaelic Irish links was underway. Participants had the opportunity to engage and debate with learned academics and to prove that conversing in Scottish Gaelic and Irish Gaelic was eminently possible, especially after a dram or two! A day or two later, we proceeded westwards by coach through the beautiful Scottish countryside to Oban to catch the ferry to the Isle of Mull. The local bus took us across Mull to Fionnport. The sun shone all the way. A golden eagle was sighted circling overhead, prompting Con to recite 'The Eagle':

> He clasps the crag with crooked hands;
> Close to the sun in lonely lands,
> Ring'd with the azure world, he stands.
>
> The wrinkled sea beneath him crawls;
> He watched from his mountain walls,
> And like a thunderbolt he falls.

From Fionnport a short ferry trip to the island across the Sound of Iona brought the travellers to their destination.

A tiny island, Iona holds a unique place in the story of Scotland and the Scottish imagination. Many thousands visit every year. Yet it's also where people have lived, worked and worshipped over many centuries. Those coming to and from its shores have included monks and pilgrims, clan chiefs and kings, artists and craftsmen, farmers and fishermen. That mid-summer day under blue skies it offered several hours of peaceful exploration and contemplation. The monastic buildings have been restored by the Iona Community and Iona Abbey is now an ecumenical church.

It is said that when the St. Columba died, his tombstone was made from the stone on which he rested his head as he slept. A stone called 'St. Columba's Pillow' was unearthed in 1870 by a crofter whose cart-wheel bumped over the stone regularly – until he finally dug it up. The stone can be seen in the Abbey museum.

As the voyagers absorbed the setting, the history and the natural beauty, a flight of white doves rose and scattered above the abbey rooftops. And then, as if summoned by a magician, Asgard II, the Irish sail training vessel, appeared on the horizon and sailed in to anchor off shore. The voyagers were rowed out to visit the vessel with the proud masthead of Granuaile, the sea queen of Connacht, and meet the captain and trainees.

It was a unique journey. Throughout, the sky seemed wondrously bright and wide, its colour more intense than possible; the sea seemed broad and deep, the air and conversation full of life, poetry and song. Con was central to the voyage and its magic. Merlin-like, he made it happen.

# RICHARD STOKES
Con And Sir Sidney Nolan

I first knew Con in the 1960s when I worked briefly in the Protocol section of the Department of External/Foreign Affairs and he was making a name for himself in the Boston consulate and at home in the Information Division. His rapport with the media was legendary.

Years later, I had contacts with him when I had responsibility for cultural matters at the Department of the Taoiseach. He had good ideas about what we should be doing in international cultural affairs. In particular he felt that we should be preparing to celebrate the Irish dimension coming up to the Australian Bicentennial. He felt that, if we didn't, the 'Brits' would dominate it.

To this end, in 1983 he established a committee under the chairmanship of Australian Susan O'Reilly (the wife of Tony O'Reilly) and I, among others, was brought into it with a specific brief to organise an exhibition of the paintings of Sir Sidney Nolan.

At his urging, I rang Nolan in Australia and got a commitment from him to have the loan of 40 of his paintings for an exhibition in Kilkenny where Con was organising a conference to celebrate Ireland – Australia in the lead up to the bicentennial.

A successful conference took place, and the Australian ambassador performed the opening ceremony, as well at the accompanying exhibition, which was much acclaimed. So much so that I felt it should be seen more widely, and it was subsequently shown at the National Concert Hall in Dublin. At the request of the Belltable Arts Centre in Limerick it was also shown there.

This was a classic example of Con's creative impetus at work. He managed to raise the necessary funds, mainly from the O'Reillys.

Con's creativity was not always matched by the necessary administrative niceties, but without his flair the venture would not have been dreamt of or got off the ground. He was a man of ideas, of a vision not always widely appreciated. He brought this creativity to bear on other projects too, such as the St. Brendan activities and the Catalpa project.

Incidentally, the Nolan exhibition gave rise to a promise from the painter of a gift of over 50 of his paintings for Ireland. Sadly Sir Sidney died soon after this but he gave several of his paintings to the Irish Museum of Modern Art (IMMA). This formed the nucleus of the Museum's collection, and brought a happy outcome to Con's bicentennial project.

# SEAN TYRRELL
## The Midnight Court

I first met Con in Washington DC in the early 1980s in a very upmarket bar and restaurant called The Ebbitt Grill – a favourite haunt of the political elite of American politics and managed by Tom Costello, a good friend of mine from Kildimo. To say that it was an entertaining night would indeed be an understatement.

Costello is one of the great raconteurs, and here I had met another – Con Howard. In the early hours of the morning, when we finally adjourned to our beds, my sides were sore with all the laughter. I still have a vivid memory of Con's over-the-top rendition of the 'Windswept Hills of Tulla' to an amazed and shell-shocked, polite, quiet DC clientele.

It would be many more years before our paths would cross again when I began my journey with *The Midnight Court*. I had set it to music and was attempting to get it staged at the Galway Arts Festival. Maoilísa Stafford, then artistic director of Druid, agreed to put it on, but we had to raise £8,000. I had heard that Con was one of the people involved in Cumann Merriman, so I approached to see if there was any way they could help us with the fundraising. No money came from Cumann Merriman but Con sent us a cheque from his own account, which I have appreciated ever since. It was not just the money, but the fact that he encouraged me with his passion and enthusiasm for the poem, and to keep *The Midnight Court* as an ongoing production. Right up to a few months before his death he continued, with his presence, to support our efforts to keep the show on the road.

We met on many occasions when he and Mary Caulfield came on their annual pilgrimage to Clare. There was always a great sense of fun and conversation on topics that roamed all over the place. From the very first night we met in DC, I was in awe of this man and his obvious charisma, and he always made me feel that what I was trying to do was important to him.

A true ambassador for Irish culture who was not afraid to swim against the tide and colour outside the confines, Con brought thousands of jobs to Ireland, many through his friendship with Mayor Daly of Chicago. What better legacy to leave to those lucky enough to cross his path than to be remembered with a smile.

# THE CONTRIBUTORS

JOHN BANVILLE, the author of 14 previous novels, has been the recipient of the Man Booker Prize, the James Tait Black Memorial Prize, the Guardian Fiction Award, a Lannan Literary Award and the Kafka Prize. Recently he is writing film scripts and crime novels under the pseudonym Benjamin Black.

JOHN BEHAN is a sculptor and artist. He studied at NCAD, Ealing Art College and Royal Academy School, Olso. He is founder of Project Arts Centre and the Dublin Art Foundry. Notable sculptures include 'Arrival' in the UN plaza and 'Wings of the World' in China. He is a member of Aosdána.

MAEVE BINCHY's first novel *Light A Penny Candle* was published in 1982. Since then she has written over 20 novels – all bestsellers. Several have been adapted for cinema and TV – most notably *Circle Of Friends*. She was awarded the Lifetime Achievement Award at the British Book Awards in 1998.

WESLEY BOYD was head of RTÉ's news division from 1972 – 1990. He was previously the diplomatic correspondent with the *Irish Times* and London editor of the Belfast daily paper *The Northern Whig*.

The late PATRICIA BOYLAN contributed essays and articles to many periodicals and newspaper, and scripts to Radió Éireann. She attended the Abbey School of Acting when Lennox Robinson was director and acted at the Abbey, Peacock and Gaiety Theatres, but mostly in broadcast plays and performances. She was a member of Lennox Robinson's select group of students chosen to keep poetry alive in the theatre and later was a founder of the Dublin Verse Speaking Society. For over 20 years she broadcast on the Austin Clarke's Weekly Poetry Night.

DOMINICK, LORD ORANMORE AND BROWNE, is a poet and playwright.

PAT BYRNE is a retired teacher and journalist. He is now concentrating on poetry and is preparing a collection of poetry for publication.

MARY CAULFIELD is a teacher and university lecturer. She lives in Dublin, where she is vice president of the United Arts Club and the Shaw Society, and founder of the Irish Byron Society. She was formerly a committee member of the Australia-Ireland Bicentennial conference, and also the Merriman Society, which published the prize-winning *America And Ireland 1776 - 1996*.

BRENDAN CONWAY is a native of Feakle, Co. Clare. He was a teacher and headmaster in the vocational educational services of the City of Dublin. He transferred to Kilkenny where he was, for over 20 years, CEO. He is a staunch member of Cumann Merriman.

ANTHONY CRONIN is a poet, novelist and biographer of Flann O'Brien and Samuel Beckett. He was Cultural Adviser to the Taoiseach CJ Haughey.

SEÁN DONLON is former Secretary General of the Department of Foreign Affairs and Ambassador of Ireland to the United States of America and to Mexico.

JAMES DOWNEY is one of Ireland's most renowned journalists. He writes a weekly political column in the *Irish Independent*. He was formerly foreign editor, London editor, political correspondent and deputy editor of the *Irish Times*. He has won several journalism awards including the Liam Hourican Award for Ireland's European Journalist of the Year in 1996.

DESMOND FENNELL is a travel writer, cultural philosopher and linguist. He was born Belfast 1929, studied history at University College Dublin and completed an MA after a year at Bonn University. In 1990, he was awarded D. Litt for his published work. He is married with five children.

SEAMUS HEANEY's first collection *Death Of A Naturalist* appeared in 1966 and since then he has written poetry, prose, criticism and translations, which have established him as one of the leading poets of his generation. He has twice won the Whitbread Book of the *Year for Spirit Level* in 1996 and Beowulf in 1999. In 1998 he was awarded the Nobel Prize for Literature. *Human Chain* is his 13th collection of poems.

MONICA HENCHY is a retired assistant librarian at TCD. She was president of the Dublin Spanish Society for several years. Her special interest is the history of the Irish colleges in Spain, on which she has lectured and written extensively.

NUALA HOGAN is a stalwart of Cumann Merriman. She loves literature and resides in Clare.

CATHERINE JENNINGS graduated in French from UCC, did postgraduate studies in the universities of Strasbourg in France and Fribourg in Switzerland, and circa 1970 was an assistant lecturer in French in UCC.

The late JOSEPH JUDGE was a native of Washington DC, where he lived all of his life. He earned an AB degree from the Catholic University of America and The Cricket Hill Press published his first book of poems in 1948. He contributed fiction to several major American magazines and spent much of his time travelling and writing for *National Geographic* magazine, of which he was the associate editor.

MORGAN LLYWELYN is author of, among others, *The Wind From Hastings, Lion of Ireland, The Horse Goddess, Druids, The Last Prince of Ireland, The Greener Shore* and *Brendán*. She has won many awards, including the 'Exceptional Celtic Woman Award' in 1999.

BRENDAN LYNCH is a freelance writer and author of six books, including *Prodigals And Geniuses – The Writers And Artists Of Dublin's Baggotonia"*.

PEADAR MAC MÁGHNAIS is a medical graduate of UCD (1960). His postgraduate work was in ophthalmology, and he worked in London, East and Central Africa. He returned to Ireland in 1971 and worked in Our Lady's Hospital for Sick Children for 33 years.

SEÁN MAC MATHÚNA hails from Kerry and writes in both Irish and English. His short story collection *The Atheist* was nominated by the Irish Arts Council for the European Literary Prize. He is the author of two short story collections and three novels. He has just completed a novel in English. His play *The Winter Thief* was produced by the Abbey Theatre in both languages.

DEREK MAHON was born in Belfast. He studied at Trinity College, Dublin and the Sorbonne, Paris. He is a member of Aosdána and has received the Irish Academy of Letters Award and the Scott Moncrieff Translation Prize. Gallery Press published *New Collected Poems* in 2011.

BRIAN MOONEY was born in Dublin. He moved to the Burren in the '60s and has now taken to poetry.

MIKE MOONEY is retired, and lives in Virginia, USA. He represented Bord na Móna and the ESB in America. His wife Maria is a poet.

DR. BRENDAN Ó CATHAOIR spent most of his working life with the *Irish Times*. He is the author of *John Blake Dillon: Young Irelander* and *Famine Diary*.

ULICK O'CONNOR is a poet, biographer, playwright, literary historian and critic. He has written plays in the Noh form and has translated Baudelaire.

AIDAN O'HARA is a broadcaster, folklorist and writer, who worked with RTÉ and the Canadian Broadcasting Corporation.

SEÁN Ó MÓRDHA is a magisterial documentary maker. He directed *Seven Ages* – a TV series documentary, *Samuel Beckett: Silence to Silence*, *Is There One Who Understands Me?* (The Work of James Joyce) and *Brian Friel And Field Day*. He also produced *Hidden History* and *Seven Ages*.

GABRIEL ROSENSTOCK is a poet, translator, haiku writer and editor. He is the author/translator of over 30 books and has translated into Irish the selected poems of Francisco X. Alarcón, Georg Trakl and Günter Grass.

ROSEMARIE ROWLEY was educated at Trinity College, Dublin, and holds degrees in Irish and English Literature and Philosophy, a diploma in Psychology and a Master of Literature degree for her work on the Irish poet Patrick Kavanagh. Rosemarie has published five books of poetry and has twice won the Epic award in the Scottish International Poetry Competition.

DESMOND RUSHE is a former drama critic and columnist with the *Irish Independent*.

ROSE RUSHE is a journalist with the *Limerick Post* and holds a BA from UCG. She is a member of St. Brendan's Society of Voyagers 1989 and Company Secretary of ADAPT services – a refuge for women and children.

BOB RYAN was PR manager with Allied Irish Banks from 1986 – 1990, editor of a revived *Dublin Opinion* and director of marketing and PR for Cerebral Palsy Ireland from 1988 – 1997. He studied art at the Crawford Municipal School of Art in Cork and the National College of Art in Dublin.

MONSIGNOR TOM STACK, a long time friend of Con's, is a priest of the archdiocese of Dublin (with Clare roots). Now retired, he has worked in parishes and hospitals in Dublin, was a member of the Radharc documentary film team and a newspaper columnist. His has published a volume on the spirituality of Patrick Kavanagh entitled *No Earthly Estate* and has been a regular attendee at gatherings of Cumann Merriman.

MARY STOKES is a psychologist and hold a masters degree in Equality Studies. She is an intrepid traveller and has travelled extensively in Europe, Asia and the Americas.

RICHARD STOKES is an Arts graduate of UCD. He is a former member of the Arts Council, a director of the National Concert Hall and assistant secretary in the Department of the Taoiseach with responsibility for arts and culture.

SEAN TYRRELL is a singer and musician. He is, at present, touring in the US.

# ACKNOWLEDGEMENTS

I am profoundly grateful to the following for their contribution to *Memories of Con Howard*: John Behan, Peadar Mac Mághnais, Mary Stokes, John Banville, Nuala Hogan, Morgan Llywelyn, Catherine Jennings, Rose Rushe, Desmond Rushe, Seamus Heaney, Derek Mahon, Rosemarie Rowley, Wesley Boyd, Pat Byrne, Seán Mac Mathúna, Mike Mooney, Gabriel Rosenstock, James Downey, Bob Ryan, Seán Ó Mordha, Sean Tyrell, Dominick Lord Oranmore and Browne, Brendan Lynch, Anthony Cronin, Richard Stokes, Maeve Binchy, Aiden O'Hara, Monsignor Tom Stack, Ulick O'Connor, Seán Donlon, Brian Mooney, Monica Henchy, Desmond Fennell, Brendan Ó Cathaoir, Brendan Conway, the widow of Joseph Judge, Phyllis, for permission to publish her husband's letter and the Boylan family and publisher Colin Smythe for permission to use an extract from Patricia's book. And I am indebted to Mick O'Dea RHA, who gave me permission to reproduce his portrait of Con, and to Maureen Comber of Clare County Library for permission to reproduce a photograph of Con taken in 1968 at Quin Abbey. The photograph was taken by John Horgan.

– Mary Caulfield